Chocolate is one of those foods that's universally loved.
But Steve Hodge—chocolatier, pastry chef and TV star—knows that it can be intimidating for home bakers. In his first book, he's here to take the mystery out of chocolate with over 100 meticulously tested recipes that will inspire home bakers of all skill levels. In these pages, you'll find ideas for:

Chocolate for Breakfast: Wake up with Chocolate Sticky Buns or White Chocolate Raspberry Scones;

Cakes, Tarts & Soufflés: Celebrate a special occasion or everyday gathering with a Dark Chocolate Cheesecake or Banana Cream Chocolate Pie;

Cookies, Squares & Bites: Make afternoon tea even nicer with Chocolate Almond Biscotti or Chocolate Raspberry Brownies;

Kid-Friendly Chocolate: Get the kids in the kitchen with Easy-Made Chocolate Bars or Milk Chocolate–Covered Caramel Apples;

Essential Fillings & Desserts: Learn the basics like Chocolate Crème Brûlée, White Chocolate Mirror Glaze or Chocolate Italian Buttercream;

And so much more!

In addition to his showstopping recipes, Steve also gives plenty of advice on buying, storing and working with chocolate. He'll show you how to temper it, how to create chocolate decorations and how to fix your desserts if something goes wrong. You'll learn how to taste chocolate and build a chocolate-based entertaining board that's sure to impress. But most importantly, you'll come away with the confidence to tackle any kind of chocolate recipe and make it your own. With *Chocolate All Day* as your guide, your favorite ingredient to eat will become your favorite to bake with as well!

Chocolate All Day

From Simple to Decadent,
100+ Recipes for Everyone's Favorite Ingredient

Chocolate All Day

Steven Hodge

appetite
by RANDOM HOUSE

Appetite by Random House® and colophon are registered trademarks of Penguin Random House LLC.

Library and Archives of Canada Cataloguing in Publication is available upon request.

ISBN: 9780525612025
eBook ISBN: 9780525612032

Cover and book design by Kelly Hill
Photography by Jamie Hodge and Jimmy Jeong
Printed in China

Published in Canada by Appetite by Random House®,
a division of Penguin Random House LLC.
www.penguinrandomhouse.ca

10 9 8 7 6 5 4 3 2 1

appetite
by RANDOM HOUSE

Penguin
Random House
Canada

For my mom

Contents

Introduction

I was born to bake. At least that's what my mom tells people. And she says that with some authority, sharing a story from her pregnancy with me to back it up. My dad was completing his Master of Business Administration at Western University just as my parents were starting their family. He got involved with a fledgling bakery and decided to buy it and nurture it back to business health, using his newfound knowledge. My mom, who was several months pregnant with me at the time, came in to help him develop a new lineup of baked goods and, as my dad put it, singlehandedly turned the business around. My mom has always loved baking everything from pies to cookies. It's something she learned from her mom while growing up. Some of my fondest memories are of watching my mom make pies, and to this day I'm still convinced she makes the most amazing pies.

As for many of you reading this book, food has been an important part of my life. It shapes the memories we have made and continue to make as a family, and it inspires the memories I'm making with my own kids, Charlie and Levi, today. Since starting my own chocolate and bakery business, I have loved playing a small role in helping other families make memories too. Whether it's enjoying an everyday moment with coffee and a croissant or celebrating a more significant event, like a wedding or an anniversary, with a signature cake, I find great joy in helping people spark conversations and spend time together. When it comes to my family, those occasions always feature chocolate, homemade baked goods, ice cream (lots of ice cream!) and, in the Hodge household, some form of alcohol.

But right now let's focus on chocolate. Chocolate seems to be one of those foods that is universally loved. When chocolate hits your palate, you can't help but get excited about what you're about to eat. But working with chocolate can be tricky if you haven't had specialized training. That's why I wrote this book. I want to strip away the complexity and teach people that chocolate doesn't have to be intimidating. I won't beat around the bush explaining the science behind each creation. I'll provide simple advice and guidance to give you the confidence to pick the right products and use the proper tools to get the best results. Most chocolate books are geared to professionals, but I wanted to create a book that anyone in the family could pick up and have fun using to create something impressive for the table.

This book includes recipes for all the things I loved eating as a kid and now, as a kid at heart, but with a twist to include chocolate. I'll show you how to weave this incredible ingredient into every meal and every event. I'll teach you how to pair chocolate with cocktails, turn it into a garnish and even how to host a chocolate-tasting party, because people are beginning to see chocolate the same way they do wine or coffee—a product with many distinctive flavors influenced by characteristics of the growing region and aspects of the production process. I want to expose you to the different features of chocolate to inspire you to experiment. I also want to give you dependable, show-stopping recipes that are designed to support your experimentation, so that you can introduce your family and friends to flavors they didn't know existed. These recipes and tips will help you create unique memories of your own.

My mom still cooks meals from scratch every day. She loves to make everyone happy and she does it effortlessly through food. She's inspired me my entire life, and that's what I'm hoping to do for others—to give you the tools to create your own memories and bond over great meals, holidays, milestones and more. Whether you're cooking or baking for your family, friends or friends who have become family, I want to help give you the confidence to master the recipes outlined in these chapters. But most of all, I want you to have fun with the people you love. Thank you for taking me along for the ride.

Steven

Let's Talk Chocolate

Buying Chocolate

Some people dismiss chocolate as simply a form of candy. But, in fact, research studies continue to suggest that cocoa has some of the most healthful properties on the planet. As with all good things that are inherently healthful, it is the additives found in chocolate products, such as sugar, that diminish their healthful effects. So that's why it is important to look for high-quality chocolate when you shop. I'll give you some tips to make it easy to select good-quality chocolate.

When I was growing up, recipes featuring chocolate meant a trip to the baking aisle for ingredients. Today there are many more options available. But regardless of where you get your chocolate, there are a few factors to keep in mind. First, be aware that there are products on the shelves labeled "chocolate" that are impostors and full of processed ingredients. Always start by looking at the nutrition facts label. Real chocolate is made by combining cocoa liquor, cocoa butter and sugar. Cocoa should always be the first ingredient listed. Other ingredients, such as oils, affect the overall quality and ultimately the healthfulness of the chocolate you select. In the baking aisle you may see chocolate labeled as unsweetened, bittersweet, semisweet, milk, dark or white. These refer to the percentage of cocoa they contain. High-quality couverture chocolate contains a higher percentage of cocoa butter, which makes it melt faster.

The percentage of a chocolate matters for a few reasons. It refers to the percentage of cocoa that comes from cocoa beans (cocoa liquor and cocoa butter), also known as cocoa mass. That percentage is calculated simply, by dividing the cocoa mass by the total weight of the chocolate bar. The higher the percentage, the more cocoa you're getting. Chocolate in the 60% range (also known as bittersweet) is ideal for snacking and is a well-balanced chocolate for baking. Generally, the higher the percentage, the more bitter-tasting the chocolate. In practice, chocolate of any percentage can be used to prepare the recipes in this book. Selecting the right chocolate is all about personal preference, but remember that the higher its percentage of chocolate, the more healthful it is and richer in antioxidants.

As you shop, keep in mind that all chocolate has a best-before date. The chocolate should be uniform in color, which tells you it has been stored properly. The chocolate should make a clean snap when broken, which indicates that it has been tempered properly. The chocolate shouldn't be visible through the packaging. It needs to be packaged properly to protect it from light and air, which may affect the quality and taste because of a process called oxidation. Also, be aware of the environment where you are

doing your buying—if the temperature is extremely warm, it can affect the chocolate. The ideal temperature to store chocolate is between 65° and 68°F.

When shopping for chocolate at the grocery store, consider staying away from the highly processed baker's chocolate in the baking aisle. Instead, take advantage of the aisle with the premium chocolates and those produced by local chocolatiers. These bars provide a great way to incorporate different flavors into your recipes. You can bake with pretty much any type of chocolate, so don't limit yourself by shopping in just one grocery aisle.

If there's a local bakery or a pastry or chocolate shop in your area, ask if they will sell you chocolate. Most use a higher-quality product, and they're often knowledgeable about the distinctive qualities of the chocolate they use. It's another way to explore the wonderful world of chocolate.

Storing Chocolate

The ideal way to store chocolate is in a cool, dry place and, once the package has been opened, in an airtight container. Cocoa butter is a delicate fat that can easily pick up the smells of other products close by and absorb moisture from the environment. Dark chocolate can be stored for up to two years if you keep it away from direct sunlight and moisture. Milk and white chocolate can be stored for up to one year. It's best not to refrigerate chocolate, because it can easily pick up smells and moisture in the fridge.

People often ask me if chocolate can be frozen. Yes, it can. I actually like eating frozen chocolate because of the coldness and bite, but my suggestion is to buy the chocolate you need in smaller quantities. The longer you hold on to chocolate without using it, the more it will lose some of its beautiful flavor. Freezing chocolate can also create problems, which I will talk about later.

Working with Chocolate

Melting Chocolate

The trick to melting chocolate like a pro is to cut it into small, evenly sized pieces (use a serrated knife) and to use gentle heat, because chocolate is delicate and can burn quickly if the temperature is too high. Here are two simple methods for melting chocolate properly:

DOUBLE-BOILER METHOD

The safest chocolate-melting method is to use a double boiler. This will allow you to adjust and control the temperature. You don't need an actual double boiler, though. Simply fill a pot with water to about one-quarter full. Place a heatproof bowl (glass or stainless steel works well) over a pot of water simmering on the stovetop over low heat. Add your chocolate to the bowl, ensuring that it's no more than half full, because you'll need room to stir the chocolate safely. As the chocolate begins to melt, gradually stir it to fully incorporate the melted parts with the solid pieces remaining.

The downside to the double-boiler method is that steam is created. Water and chocolate don't mix. Water can change the texture of your chocolate from silky smooth to a gritty paste, which will negatively impact your final product. To avoid this, be careful when removing the chocolate from the bowl. Make sure you have a cloth handy to wipe the water off the bottom of the bowl as well.

MICROWAVE METHOD

The second method for melting chocolate is using a microwave. This is my favorite method because it's fast. But this technique is also a little more dangerous—it's not as easy to control the heat generated by a microwave, which makes it easier to burn the chocolate. If you burn your chocolate, you can't use it, so it's important to pay close attention during the melting process.

To melt chocolate in the microwave, place chocolate pieces in a heatproof, microwave-safe bowl, being sure not to fill it more than one-quarter full. Start your microwaving with 30 seconds at medium power. Remove the bowl from the microwave and give the chocolate a stir. Continue to microwave and stir in 15-second increments until all the pieces are melted. If you have a few stubborn pieces left near the end of the process, you can move to increments of 3 to 5 seconds to ensure that you don't burn the chocolate.

Tempering Chocolate

A few of the recipes in this book call for tempered chocolate. Tempering is a process of heating and then cooling chocolate to make it more stable for use and to give it a smooth, glossy finish. If you've ever had a chocolate-covered strawberry or chocolate bonbon, you may have noticed its shiny finish and that it doesn't easily melt in your hand. That's what happens with properly tempered chocolate. Higher-quality chocolates have more cocoa butter content and are therefore a little easier to handle in a process such as tempering.

There are several ways to temper chocolate, and I'll give you two techniques. I won't dive into the science behind the process, but I do want to share the three important steps required to temper chocolate at home in a straightforward way. Every different type and percentage of chocolate reaches temper at a different temperature, but the basic technique applies to dark, milk, white and ruby chocolates. Some chocolate packages include a tempering grid, and I've also included one below (page 9) that you can follow for all types of chocolate. You'll need a thermometer for this process; you can find some recommmendations in the tools section (page 19).

TABLE TEMPERING TECHNIQUE

Once you've melted your chocolate, the first step in the tempering process is to bring the unstable fatty acids of the cocoa butter back to a stable form. To do this, you need to heat the chocolate to the temperature listed in Step 1 of the tempering grid below. I've described two ways of melting chocolate above (page 7), but the double-boiler method is easiest for this process.

Once it reaches the temperature in Step 1, pour two-thirds of the melted chocolate onto a clean, dry, cool surface. A marble countertop works particularly well, as does granite—smooth stone slabs are great for keeping the chocolate cool but still malleable. Once you've poured the chocolate, use a kitchen scraper to keep it moving in a figure-eight motion. The chocolate will thicken.

Once the chocolate reaches the temperature listed in Step 2 of the grid, you can pour it back in with the rest of the melted chocolate. Mix well and it's ready to use. The chocolate should look smooth and shiny.

SEEDING TECHNIQUE

The seeding method for tempering chocolate is easy and fast. First, chop the chocolate into pieces that are smaller than a nickel. Next, melt three-quarters of the chopped chocolate in a double boiler until it reaches the Step 1 temperature listed in the tempering grid.

Remove the bowl of melted chocolate from the pot and transfer about one-third of the chocolate to a separate bowl; reserve. Add the remaining cut-up chocolate to the first bowl of melted chocolate and stir until it reaches the Step 2 temperature listed in the tempering grid.

Finally, pour the reserved melted chocolate back into the bowl. The difference in temperature between it and the melted chocolate in the first bowl should bring the full mixture to the temperature listed in Step 3.

Tempering may seem tedious, but trust me, you'll love the result. This is a process that professional chocolatiers work hard to master. Regardless of the technique you choose, it's worth the effort.

	CHOCOLATE TEMPERING GRID			
Step	**Dark Chocolate**	**Milk Chocolate**	**White Chocolate**	**Ruby Chocolate**
1	122°–131°F (50°–55°C)	113°–122°F (45°–50°C)	113°F–122°F (45°–50°C)	113°F–122°F (45°–50°C)
2	82°–84°F (28°–29°C)	81°–82°F (27°–28°C)	79°–81°F (26°–27°C)	79°–81°F (26°–27°C)
3	88°–90°F (31°–32°C)	84°–86°F (29°–30°C)	82°–84°F (28°–29°C)	82°–84°F (28°–29°C)

Cocoa Powder

Cocoa powder is a key ingredient in many of the recipes you'll find here. It's made primarily from cocoa solids and 10–12% cocoa butter. Chocolate, on the other hand, contains about 55% cocoa butter. That cocoa-solids-to-cocoa-butter ratio means that cocoa powder packs an intense chocolate punch.

There are two types of cocoa powder: natural cocoa powder and natural cacao powder. A variety of brands of both types are available. Brands with a higher fat content tend to produce baked items that are richer, tastier and more tender.

NATURAL COCOA POWDER

Natural cocoa powder is made from cacao beans that are fermented, dried and roasted at a high temperature, then cracked into nibs. The nibs are pressed to remove about 75% of the cocoa butter, leaving the chocolate liquor, which is dried and ground into cocoa powder.

Natural *cacao* powder, on the other hand, is made from fermented cacao beans that have not been roasted. The beans are processed at a lower temperature, which helps them retain more nutrients, minerals and enzymes. It is considered a raw product and has more of chocolate's bitter and acidic flavors. Cacao powder is becoming increasingly popular because of its rich nutrient content.

There are several types of unsweetened natural cocoa powder. They have different colors and tastes, and each type performs differently in recipes.

Natural cocoa powder is the most commonly used cocoa powder in North America. It is usually labeled "unsweetened" or "pure" cocoa powder. Because it is acidic, it is relatively light in color and effective in recipes that use baking soda. The acidity triggers a chemical reaction when the powder is mixed with baking soda, lifting and lightening the finished treat. Baking soda neutralizes the acidity of natural cocoa powder, which has a pH level of between 5.3 and 5.8.

Dutch-process cocoa powder

Dutch-process or alkalized cocoa powder was created by a chemist who discovered that cacao processed with an alkali solution has a much less bitter taste, because its acidity is neutralized to a pH of 7. Generally more popular in Europe, this cocoa powder is darker in color, with a smoother taste. Dutch-process cocoa powder requires baking powder as a leavener, rather than baking soda, because its acidity has already been neutralized. Baked goods made with it generally don't rise as high as those made with natural cocoa powder, but the items are more tender or fudgy.

Black cocoa powder

Black cocoa powder is a highly processed Dutch-process cocoa powder that is ultra-smooth and dark in color. It's not bitter, but it doesn't taste much like chocolate. It is best used with regular Dutch-process cocoa powder to add more flavor. Black cocoa powder is used primarily for pre-sentation purposes, to make the finished product look darker—think of that classic sandwich cookie with the white filling. Black cocoa powder has almost no fat, which results in drier, more crumbly baked items unless you add fat to the recipe to compensate. Black cocoa powder will not react with baking soda.

Red cocoa powder

Red cocoa powder is an unsweetened cocoa powder used by professional pastry chefs because of its deep red color and higher fat content, which makes it rich in flavor.

Chocolate Cuts and Garnishes

Your recipe will generally indicate the specific form
of chocolate required. Here is a quick and easy
reference to the standard terms.

ROUGH-CHOPPED
A serrated knife is easier to push through chocolate bars for a rough chop.

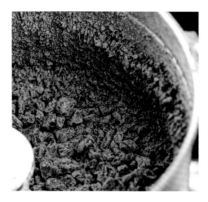

FINELY CHOPPED
Pulsing the chocolate in a food processor is perfect for fine chopping, but don't overdo it or the friction of the blade can melt the chocolate.

UNIFORM CUT
All the pieces are the same size.

GRATED CHOCOLATE
Use a Microplane grater to grate chocolate onto the plate or over a dessert.

CHOCOLATE SHAVINGS
Carefully, using a vegetable peeler, scrape along a bar of chocolate to create shavings. Use a smooth motion away from you, to avoid accidents. The chocolate should be room temperature but not warm.

CHOCOLATE CURLS
Spread a thin, even layer of tempered chocolate onto a marble board. Allow the chocolate to set slightly. Place a flexible metal bench scraper or a drywall putty knife on a 45-degree angle to the chocolate and push the chocolate away from you until it has fully and tightly curled in on itself.

MELTED CHOCOLATE
Use the techniques described on page 7 to melt the chocolate in a way that works for your recipe.

Fun Chocolate Decor

You can create finishing touches for your desserts that will impress dinner-party guests and take your special-event menu up a notch.

Here are a few chocolate decor ideas.

***** CHOCOLATE SOIL

This is a great garnish for plated desserts. It gives an earthy look that will have people wondering how you made it, and the answer is malto-dextrin—a food ingredient made from vegetable starch. It also makes a cool dessert dirt. Mix maltodextrin with melted chocolate to dry out the fat in the chocolate and leave it looking like rich soil. You may never have heard of maltodextrin, but it's easy to find online or in specialty shops.

+ CHOCOLATE IN VODKA

Create chocolate "noodles" by placing melted tempered chocolate in a piping bag, without a tip. Cut a small hole in the end of the bag. Pipe the tempered chocolate into a bowl of vodka that has been chilled in the fridge or freezer for at least 20 minutes. It will harden immediately and create chocolate that looks like noodles or string. You can pipe different shapes or create a bird's nest. This gives desserts great height, adds texture and can be part of an abstract art design.

+ ANTI-GRAVITY CHOCOLATE

Give your plates a three-dimensional perspective. Pipe a dollop of tempered chocolate onto a flat plate or piece of glass. Flip the plate upside down and press on the dollop with a spatula, then slowly pull the plate away, creating drips of chocolate. Secure the plate upside down by resting it on the rim of a bowl or pot until the chocolate drips have set. This is a fun way to artistically plate a dessert, within and around the chocolate.

+ SWIRLS

These chocolate swirls are easy and fun to make, and give a high-end feel to your desserts. Spread tempered chocolate evenly along a marble slab with an offset spatula. Place a flexible metal bench scraper or a drywall putty knife on a 45-degree angle to the chocolate and push the chocolate away from you, diagonally, to create the swirl.

+ LEAVES

Create a wilderness from chocolate. Place a large piece of acetate or parchment paper on your work surface, right to the edge. Pipe a small button-sized dollop of chocolate 1½ inches from the edge of the work surface. Using a flat, pointed narrow knife or a flat, pointed, narrow palette knife, press it flat onto the chocolate. Push the knife forward, away from you, keeping light pressure on the chocolate to create the tip of the leaf. Then pull the knife back toward you, and slide it right off the table. Before the chocolate sets completely, create its shape by placing it into a curved mold.

+ BALLOON CUP

Make your very own dessert cups of any size to hold your sweets. Blow up a balloon to the size that you'd like your chocolate bowl to be. Place tempered chocolate in a bowl, and dip the round part of the balloon into the bowl about one-quarter of the way up. Remove, rotate the balloon 180 degrees and dip again. Immediately place the balloon, standing upright, on a sheet of parchment paper to set. When you're ready to use the chocolate bowl, take a needle and gently pop the balloon so the chocolate doesn't break. Carefully peel the balloon off.

+ CHOCOLATE HAY

Use chocolate hay to build nests or to give height to the desserts you prepare. Take a metal rolling pin, metal canister, or anything metal in the shape of a cylinder, and chill it in the freezer for 10 minutes. Temper your chocolate and transfer to a piping bag with a small hole cut at the bottom. Remove the metal cylinder from the freezer, place it on parchment paper and quickly pipe lines of chocolate across the cylinder. The chocolate will set due to the coldness of the metal. Immediately slide the chocolate right off onto the parchment, using your fingers, but don't touch the chocolate any further until fully set.

+ CHOCOLATE FANS

Spread tempered chocolate on a marble slab with an offset spatula until semi-set. Using a flexible bench scraper, place your thumb in the middle of the scraper, right at the edge. With the scraper at a 45-degree angle to the marble slap, and keeping pressure on the chocolate, make a fan movement as you scrape the chocolate up. There are some great YouTube videos that show this technique.

* EASY CHOCOLATE MOLDING CLAY

Build your own showpieces for the holiday table or use chocolate molding clay to create flowers or other shapes.

Step 1: Place some chopped chocolate in a food processor and pulse until the chocolate is warm and pliable.

Step 2: Knead the chocolate until it comes together. The warmth of your hands will allow you to work with it.

Step 3: Form the chocolate into your desired shape—swirls, flowers, animals, etc. Let cool completely to set and harden, then use as decor.

+ CHOCOLATE MARBLE BOARD

Step 1: Place a piece of parchment paper on a baking sheet with a metal cake ring on top. Sprinkle different types of chocolate in the bottom of the cake ring.

Step 2: Pour tempered chocolate over the solid pieces to about ¼ inch thick. Let set for 30 minutes at room temperature, or for 10 minutes in the fridge.

Step 3: Remove the metal ring. Heat a metal baking sheet or pot in the oven. Place the slab of chocolate on the heated surface, with the chocolate pieces (the bottom side) directly on the metal.

Step 4: Slowly make circular motions to slightly melt the base of the chocolate, then transfer to a work surface.

Step 5: Using a metal bench scraper, gently scrape the melted surface of the chocolate to remove it.

Step 6: Like magic, the chocolate pieces will appear and you'll have your chocolate marble board.

Recovering If Something Goes Wrong

Just like everything in life, sometimes, despite our best efforts, baking goes wrong. I'm here to tell you that chocolate is surprisingly forgiving. If you make a misstep, you can just start all over again. Chocolate can be melted down and reused, so don't worry about making mistakes.

FAT BLOOM

Have you ever purchased a chocolate bar that has a dull, grayish-looking film? That's what we professionals call fat bloom. It happens if chocolate isn't stored properly and has been exposed to heat or hasn't been tempered properly. Fat bloom results when the cocoa butter separates from the crystallized chocolate and then solidifies on the surface of the chocolate, creating streaks of gray. Storing chocolate in a cool place is important to prevent blooming. Once your chocolate has a fat bloom, there's no getting rid of it.

SUGAR BLOOM

A sugar bloom looks like white streaks on the chocolate surface and occurs when chocolate is exposed to moisture. The sugar crystals melt and rise to the top, forming a white crystalline layer on the chocolate. The sugar absorbs moisture, dissolves and then evaporates, leaving a sandpapery feel on the surface of the chocolate.

While bloomed chocolate of both types has a less than stellar appearance, and the taste and texture may be altered, it is safe to cook with and eat. You can also remelt the chocolate and temper it again. This is another reason why I love chocolate—it's so versatile. Your chocolate mistake can play a new role as chocolate garnish or, as I like to say, chocolate decor. It can also be chopped up and used in baked items such as chocolate chip cookies and cakes, or even for ice-cream desserts.

A Baker's Dozen Chocolate Tools

People create tools for good reasons! The right tool makes the workload easier, helps you become more productive and makes the job more fun. Making a small investment in the proper tools will pay off with more consistent outcomes for your baked goods. Here is a baker's dozen of basic chocolate tools to consider adding to your pantry.

WHISK

A whisk is one of the most versatile tools in the kitchen. You can use it to beat eggs and cream and fold mousse mixtures. There are many different styles on the market. I recommend starting with a basic French or all-purpose whisk. This tool takes a beating, so look for one with sturdy but thin, flexible wire hoops that create movement when you're whisking ingredients.

DIGITAL THERMOMETER

A thermometer is one of the most important tools to own if you're making chocolate desserts or tempering chocolate. It is also essential for making caramel, toffee or fudge. There are many types of thermometers on the market, but I recommend investing in a good-quality digital thermometer, because it will measure temperature faster and more accurately and it's safer to use than a traditional thermometer.

SCALE

I always have a scale in my kitchen to measure ingredients by weight, and you'll see that most recipes in this book include gram measurements as well as spoon and cup. I highly recommend using a scale rather than measuring spoons and cups for baking. Chocolate comes in many forms, from bars and chips to powder and pailletés, and it is important to use a scale to measure it, and other ingredients too. One of the secrets to success in baking is accurate measurements, and a scale gives you the best results. Digital scales are inexpensive, widely available and easy to clean and store.

DOUBLE BOILER

There are a few different methods for melting and tempering chocolate, but the double-boiler method I describe on page 7 is the safest. There are many double boilers available to purchase, but you can also create your own by placing a heatproof bowl over a pot of simmering water.

SILICONE SPATULA

Every kitchen should have a good-quality spatula. It's especially handy for getting chocolate out of the bowl. Chocolate is expensive, so you want to use every little bit. Today's silicone spatulas are more durable than rubber spatulas, and they can withstand higher temperatures.

GLASS BOWLS

Heatproof bowls are a must for melting chocolate in the microwave or over a pot on the stove as part of a double boiler. Get a set of glass bowls to use for everything from mixing and melting to proofing dough and storing leftovers.

IMMERSION BLENDER

Emulsifying is a common practice in baking and cooking. Essentially it's the process of bringing two ingredients together that don't typically mix. An electric immersion blender makes emulsifying ganache, fillings and creams much easier than doing it by hand with a whisk or a spatula.

DIPPING FORKS

These special forks are the perfect tool for dipping chocolate and confections into tempered chocolate. They are also great for adding clean, precise finishing touches to your chocolates or desserts. You can easily find inexpensive dipping forks through a specialty store or online retailer.

MARBLE SLAB

Marble boards are cool to the touch, and great for helping to set ganache and candy confections with flat bottoms. Marble does a great job of pulling heat from chocolate and speeding up its setting time. It is also used in the table tempering technique. You don't have to redesign your kitchen—just purchase a marble cutting board.

STAND MIXER

While a stand mixer can be pricy, it's worth the investment. It will allow you to work more efficiently, giving you more time to enjoy the results.

OFFSET SPATULAS

These are handy tools for expertly spreading mousse, icing or ganache to achieve a beautifully flat, even surface. They are also a key tool when table tempering chocolate, to create movement while helping you work.

FOOD PROCESSOR

This is a must-have tool in the kitchen. Not only is it great for chopping up chocolate and saving time, but you can also chop nuts, dried fruit or cold butter and even emulsify certain things, such as chocolate ganache. A food processor also provides a quick and easy way to make pâte brisée and tart doughs.

SILICONE MOLDS

Start your collection of differently shaped silicone molds and baking will become fun, I guarantee it. You can create shapes for baking, but you can also use these molds to shape chocolate and to freeze mousse, ice cream and ganache for toppers on cakes. There are endless opportunities.

ADDITIONAL BASICS TO COMPLETE THE PANTRY

Measuring spoons	Cookie cutters
Dry measuring cups	Baking sheets
Rolling pin	Cake pans in various sizes
Mesh sifters	Silicone pastry mats
Wire racks	Cookie scoops in a
Bench scraper	variety of sizes
Serrated knife	Pastry brushes
Chef's knife	Piping tips

Digital Thermometer, Scale

Immersion Blender, Glass Bowl, Pots

Silicone Spatula, Measuring Cups and Spoons, Mesh Sifter

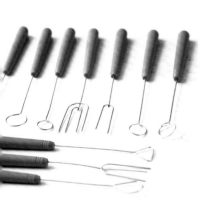

Dipping Forks

Marble Slab, Cutting Boards

Stand Mixer

Offset Spatulas

Silicone Molds

Bench Scrapers, Cookie Cutter, Silicone Mold, Silicone Pastry Mat, Piping Tips

Tasting Chocolate

Hosting a chocolate-tasting party is as wonderful as the name suggests. Just as parties for wine tasting or beer tasting that feature cheese and charcuterie boards are both fun and delicious experiences, diving into the rich tastes of chocolates from a variety of cocoa regions is a decadent experience.

Your tasting board can be inspired by the seasons, the chocolate bars you profile and the ingredients you have on hand. Think of the board as your story or song sheet. What will be your beginning, middle and end? The individual elements will work together to create the plot or the music.

Start the tasting journey with sweeter chocolates and end with bitter chocolates. Incorporate chocolates with texture (nuts, fruits or melted chocolate) and add a variety of items that will help you isolate flavor notes in the chocolate itself, such as raspberries. Add items that pair well with chocolate, such as bananas or apricots (see more about pairings on page 26).

You can share the duties by supplying the chocolate and inviting your guests to bring complementary items such as fruits, nuts or cheese. Yes, cheese! I know, it sounds wild, right? But have you ever tried Parmigiano-Reggiano, goat cheese or even a sharp blue cheese with chocolate? How about making a goat-cheese chocolate ganache for the tasting board? That's the amazing thing about chocolate: it pairs well with so many other items.

Tune in to your five senses to guide the experience. First, focus on sight. Look at the chocolate—its shine and color. Beans from every cacao crop produce different colors, from reddish to dark brown. Listen to the snap of the chocolate as you break off a piece to taste. A crisp snap means the chocolate has been properly tempered.

Once you've broken off a piece, smell the chocolate. Rub it with your thumb to warm it up and then smell it again to catch the fragrances released. Focus to see if you can pick out specific notes, such as floral, nutty, fruity or earthy scents.

Next is everyone's favorite: taste. Place the chocolate on your tongue and pause as it slowly melts. What flavor notes are released? Does the flavor continue to rise in intensity and linger, or does it pack a punch and then quickly dissipate? Once you've swallowed the chocolate, has the flavor changed? What notes linger?

Pairing adds complexity. How does the taste profile of the chocolate change when paired with foods that add texture or complementary flavors, such as nuts or berries, for example? Do certain flavors in the chocolate stand out more when you introduce other foods? Does the texture of the chocolate change when paired with items that have different textures? Does it seize in your mouth or does it melt in your mouth?

For the sense of touch, focus on studying the texture of the chocolate once it's in your mouth. Is it silky or gritty? Texture is an important mark of quality. Good-quality chocolate, in which the cocoa butter has been evenly distributed during processing (called "conching"), delivers a smooth finish on your tongue. What do you notice about the texture as it changes from solid to liquid? How would you describe the mouthfeel?

Extend the chocolate board you've assembled to your glass or cup—consider serving chocolate as a drink. Think about making a hot chocolate with warming chilies, adding chocolate to your favorite tea or mixing up a chocolate martini with vodka.

Don't limit yourself to just one type of chocolate. Explore the different tastes and aromas of dark, milk, white and ruby chocolates from a variety of producers. Think about which foods pair best with each type. I love the taste of dark chocolate with acidic fruit. My kids love milk chocolate with nuts, and my friends like white chocolate with blackberries and ruby chocolate with sharp cheddar cheese. The most important thing to remember is that there are no rules. Taste is subjective. Have fun exploring and talking with your friends about the subtleties of chocolate.

Chocolate Art

As you read and make the recipes throughout this book, you'll notice that at the beginning of each chapter, there is art. But you might not realize that this art wasn't made from paint. All the chapter opener art images use real chocolate and cocoa butter, with food coloring, and we use this art on the packaging at my Vancouver pastry shop, Temper Chocolate & Pastry, as well.

The most basic way to create your own chocolate art is to start with a piece of acetate paper as your canvas (you can also use waxed paper if you don't have acetate). Paint on your designs using cocoa butter mixed with the food coloring of your choice, brush on different colors of chocolate, and let it set for 30 minutes at room temperature. While it sets, temper some chocolate. Spread the tempered chocolate overtop of your art, and let it set in the fridge for 10 minutes. Once set, remove it from the fridge, flip it over and peel off the acetate paper.

Let your mind roam free, think outside of the box and push your chocolate skills to the next level. You'll become more comfortable working with chocolate and the process will become more gratifying too. Because, at the end of the day, the best part about chocolate is enjoying it, understanding it and having fun with it.

Chocolate Pairings

Throughout this book I use several types of chocolate. Today there are wonderful companies that produce amazing varieties. Each producer has their own style and flavor profile, so I encourage you to taste a few varieties to determine which you enjoy the most. Just as with wine, the flavor of chocolate is influenced by its geographic region, the crops growing nearby and the processing techniques. I love tasting different chocolates and I seek out local chocolatiers wherever I go, but I have a few favorites I turn to for specific recipes. With so many options available, you will find something to match your own preferences and mood.

The flavor of chocolate can be enhanced by pairing it with other foods. Below are some suggestions and combinations that I often turn to. Before pairing chocolate, it's important to taste it on its own to determine what flavor notes are prominent. Chocolate can be fruity, nutty, spicy, acidic, bitter or earthy. Pick a food to pair with it that you feel will make the inherent notes of the chocolate pop.

On the opposite page you'll find a few pairing flavors for each of the four chocolates. Indulge and explore to discover the pairings you like best. Use the Tasting Chocolate section on page 23 to host your own tasting party. Invite friends over and guess what chocolate and pairings they might like best. This is the exciting world of chocolate— the taste, experience and preferences are different for everyone.

Ruby Chocolate

Ruby chocolate has an acidic flavor profile. The taste is slightly sweet-and-sour, with hints of berry. It pairs well with both unusual and common flavors. Here are a few to get you started:

SPICES: cinnamon, clove, ginger, matcha, wasabi

NUTS: almonds, cashews, hazelnuts, peanuts, macadamias, pecans, pistachios, walnuts

FRUITS: blackberries, blueberries, cherries, cranberries, currants, raspberries, strawberries, oranges, lemons, apples, passionfruit, mangos, lychees, kiwis, pomegranates, gooseberries, cherries

HERBS: basil, mint, rosemary, thyme

Milk Chocolate

Milk chocolate is both sweet and creamy, making it the most popular of all chocolate types. The mouthfeel is smooth and rich, and it melts in your mouth quickly. Milk chocolate has a buttery aroma, with hints of vanilla, malt and caramel.

SPICES: chai, cardamom, toasted sesame, ginger, lavender, cinnamon

NUTS: almonds, pecans, peanuts, walnuts

FRUITS: apples, bananas, cherries, pears, strawberries, raspberries, apricots, mangos, passion fruit, coconuts

OTHER: caramel, honey

White Chocolate

White chocolate does not contain cocoa solids and is typically flavored with vanilla, which lends a soft floral note to the final finish. It is more subtle and delicate in flavor than the bold profile of dark chocolate. White chocolate is also higher in cocoa butter, which gives it a creamier and silkier feel in the mouth.

SPICES: cardamom, saffron, matcha, cayenne, black sesame, lavender, ginger, sea salt

NUTS: macadamias, cashews, hazelnuts

FRUITS: lemons, limes, oranges, blueberries, cranberries, blackberries, raspberries, passionfruit, yuzu, coconuts

HERBS: lemongrass

OTHER: caramel

Dark Chocolate

Dark chocolate has the most wide-ranging and complex flavor profiles, which vary with the chocolate percentage and the growing region. You can pick up sweet, sour, bitter, fruity and nutty notes.

SPICES: cardamom, cayenne pepper, chili, cinnamon, fennel, ginger, curry, sea salt

NUTS: hazelnuts, almonds, pecans, peanuts

FRUITS: bananas, apricots, raspberries, black currants, blackberries, cherries, lemons, oranges, mangos, passionfruit, grapes

OTHER: caramel, coffee

Some Notes on Ingredients

Before you indulge in these recipes, I want to share key notes on some of the ingredients that I use.

Chocolate Types

You will see that when a recipe calls for dark chocolate, milk chocolate or white chocolate, no percentages are typically indicated. These recipes were built to explore the different types of chocolate you can use. For example, whether you want to use a 60% or 70% chocolate, the recipe will work. Keep in mind, though, that the higher the percentage of cocoa mass, the less sweet the dish will be.

Cocoa Powder

You will see that I mostly use Dutch-process cocoa powder. I prefer this type because it is darker in color and less bitter, and it produces baked goods that are more tender and fudgy. I use baking powder more often than baking soda, as Dutch-process cocoa powder requires baking powder as a leavening agent. But you can experiment. If you do not have Dutch-process cocoa powder, use a different type and see how the recipe works. It will still taste great, but let's see if you can spot the differences in texture and appearance. Have fun with that!

Gelatin

I will not get into the science of gelatin, but you will see that the recipes include both sheet and powdered gelatin as options. I've given both so you can use whichever one you're able to purchase. Gelatin comes in different strengths, meaning some have more bloom power than others. For example, in leaf form, you can get titanium, which has a bloom strength of 120. Bronze has a strength of 140, silver has 160, gold has 200 and platinum has 250. The recipes in this book were tested with gold gelatin sheets that have a bloom strength of 200. Keep in mind that if you're going to interchange types, the general rule for 200 gold bloom strength is 1 sheet gold bloom strength per 2 grams gelatin powder called for.

When blooming gelatin, use cold water. If the water is warm, you will melt the gelatin and not be able to use it. The ratio for gelatin sheets is 1 sheet per 1 cup (250 ml) cold water; allow it to soak for up to 5 minutes. The ratio for gelatin powder is 1 part powder to 5 parts water; allow the gelatin to absorb the water for up to 8 minutes. The hydrated gelatin should look and feel like a soft puck, and you should be able to remove it from the bowl in one piece.

Chocolate
for Breakfast

Chocolate Waffles with Macerated Strawberries

Makes 6 waffles
Prep Time: 15 minutes
Cook Time: 30 minutes

Macerated Strawberries

10 fresh strawberries (370 g)

2 tablespoons (25 g) granulated sugar

Whipped Cream

1 cup (250 ml) heavy cream

2 tablespoons (16 g) icing sugar

Waffles

2 cups (290 g) all-purpose flour

⅓ cup (40 g) Dutch-process cocoa powder

1 tablespoon (9 g) baking powder

½ teaspoon kosher salt

3 large eggs, separated

1½ cups (375 ml) whole milk

6½ tablespoons (80 g) granulated sugar

⅓ cup (75 g) unsalted butter, melted

3 oz (85 g) dark chocolate, chopped

Grated dark chocolate (see page 13), for garnish

Waffles are a breakfast staple in our family. When I was growing up, I looked forward to our Sunday morning family brunch. My dad made waffles with fresh strawberries and whipped cream. I've continued this sweet tradition with my kids, but I like to give my waffles a few twists. Macerating the strawberries sweetens and tenderizes the berries, which helps them balance perfectly with the bitterness of the chocolate I add to the batter.

1. Slice the strawberries into uniform pieces and place in a bowl. Sprinkle the sugar over the strawberries and stir to mix. Cover the bowl with plastic wrap and place in the fridge for 10 minutes.

2. For the whipped cream, whisk together the cream and icing sugar to medium peaks, either by hand with a whisk or using a stand mixer on medium speed. Place in the fridge until ready to use.

3. Preheat your waffle machine.

4. In a bowl, sift together the flour, cocoa powder, baking powder and salt.

5. Place the egg yolks and milk in a separate bowl and whisk together.

6. Place the egg whites in a large bowl or the bowl of your stand mixer, along with the sugar. Whisk with an electric hand mixer or in the bowl of the stand mixer until stiff peaks form, about 3 minutes.

7. Combine the flour mixture with the egg yolk mixture and whisk together until fully incorporated. Make sure the batter is smooth. Fold the egg whites into the batter to incorporate fully. Fold in the melted butter, followed by the chopped chocolate.

8. Use a 3-ounce ladle or ice-cream scoop to portion the batter into the waffle iron, and follow your machine's cooking directions.

9. To serve, garnish the waffles with the macerated strawberries, whipped cream and grated chocolate.

Chocolate Bananas Foster Croatian Palačinke Crêpes

Makes ten 8-inch crêpes
Prep Time: 15 minutes
Cook Time: 25 minutes

Crêpes

1 cup (150 g) all-purpose flour

⅓ cup (40 g) Dutch-process cocoa powder

¼ cup (60 g) unsalted butter, melted

3½ tablespoons (45 g) granulated sugar

1 cup (250 ml) whole milk

½ cup (125 ml) soda water

1 teaspoon kosher salt

2 large eggs

Banana Filling

½ cup (115 g) unsalted butter, room temperature

½ cup (100 g) dark brown sugar

¼ teaspoon ground cinnamon

2 tablespoons (30 ml) water

1 tablespoon (15 ml) vanilla extract

¼ cup (60 ml) heavy cream

2 tablespoons (30 ml) dark rum

6 large bananas

Whipped cream, for garnish

I absolutely love crêpes. While they originated in France, there are a variety of crêpe styles throughout Europe. My mom is Croatian, so we grew up making a Croatian version of crêpes called palačinke. They're just like French crêpes but we use soda water to lighten the batter. They've become a go-to staple for breakfast, lunch or dinner in our house because they're so versatile. You can make them sweet or savory, and you can roll them, fold them or stack them.

1. First make the crêpe batter. Combine the flour, cocoa powder, melted butter, sugar, milk, soda water, salt and eggs in a blender. Mix on high speed until fully incorporated. Strain into a container and allow the batter to relax in the fridge for 10 minutes. If you do not have a blender, you can use an immersion blender or a whisk.

2. To make the banana filling, melt the butter in a pot set over medium heat. Add the brown sugar, cinnamon, water, vanilla extract, cream and rum. Bring to a simmer for 1 minute, then remove the pan from the heat and set aside.

3. Peel and slice the bananas and set aside.

4. Preheat an 8-inch crêpe pan over medium heat, and spray the pan with a nonstick spray. You must respray the pan after each crêpe so they do not stick.

5. Use a 2-ounce ladle or ¼-cup measure to portion the batter into the pan. Start by pouring it into the middle of the pan, then swirl the pan in a circular motion to evenly distribute the batter across the whole surface. Cook the crêpe until the batter is not too runny on the surface, about 1 minute. Then flip the crêpe, cook for about 10 seconds and remove from the pan. Repeat until you've used all the batter, remembering to spray the pan between each crêpe.

6. Once all the crêpes are ready, reheat the brown sugar mixture over low heat. Add the sliced bananas and cook for a few minutes until the bananas are warm and coated in the sauce. Spoon a few tablespoons of the banana mixture into each crêpe and then roll up the crêpes. Serve with chocolate ice cream or whipped cream, drizzled with any remaining brown sugar mixture.

NOTE

Cook the bananas during the last few minutes to prevent them from becoming mushy. You want them to keep their firm texture.

Chocolate Sticky Buns

Makes 18 sticky buns
Prep Time: 3 hours
Cook Time: 50 minutes

Brioche Dough

2½ cups (375 g) bread flour

2½ cups (375 g) all-purpose flour

½ cup (100 g) granulated sugar

2 teaspoons kosher salt

²⁄₃ cup (160 ml) whole milk

1½ tablespoons (13 g) active
 dry yeast

6 large eggs

1¾ cups (400 g) unsalted butter,
 room temperature

Filling

6 oz (170 g) milk chocolate,
 chopped

6 oz (170 g) dark chocolate,
 chopped

½ cup (114 g) unsalted butter,
 room temperature

1 cup (200 g) dark brown sugar

2 teaspoons ground cinnamon

Topping

1½ cups (336 g) unsalted butter,
 room temperature

1½ cups + 2 tablespoons (325 g)
 dark brown sugar

2 tablespoons (40 g) dark
 corn syrup

¼ cup + 2 tablespoons (90 ml)
 water

2 teaspoons Dutch-process
 cocoa powder

We all know the satisfaction that comes from biting into a really good sticky bun or cinnamon bun. I have fond memories of going to the bakery to get sticky buns early in the morning, when they were fresh out of the oven, soft and delicious. Everyone makes them a little differently. The key to a perfect sticky bun lies in the dough. I find that most sticky buns dry out quickly after they're baked, but these gooey, sweet buns stay moist. I've incorporated one of my favorite doughs, a brioche dough, which is full of flavor and rich in butter, to keep the bun tender long after it's out of the oven.

1. For the brioche dough, combine the bread flour, all-purpose flour, sugar and salt in the bowl of a stand mixer fitted with the dough hook.

2. Warm the milk slightly in a bowl in the microwave for 45 seconds or until warm to the touch, then add the yeast. Whisk together so the yeast dissolves. Next, whisk the eggs into the milk.

3. Slowly pour the milk-and-egg mixture into the dry ingredients. Mix the dough on low speed until it comes together, about 10 minutes.

4. Once the dough has formed, add the room-temperature butter to the mixing bowl. Increase the speed to medium and mix until the butter is fully incorporated and the dough is separating from the sides of the bowl. The dough should be smooth and shiny.

5. Remove the dough from the mixing bowl and place on a floured work surface. Give the dough 5 kneaded folds to bring it together. Place the dough on a floured baking sheet, lightly cover the top with plastic wrap and let it relax in the fridge for 1 hour.

6. Meanwhile, make the filling. Place the chopped milk and dark chocolates in a microwave-safe bowl and melt in the microwave (see page 7). Set aside.

7. Combine the butter, brown sugar and cinnamon in a pot over low heat and melt them together. Then, using a spatula, add the melted chocolate and stir to fully combine. Set aside to cool.

8. Then make the topping. Melt the butter in a small pot set over medium heat. Add the brown sugar, corn syrup, water and cocoa powder and bring to a simmer to melt and combine. Pour the mixture into a 12-inch round skillet or a 12-inch square baking dish. Set aside to cool.

9. Once the dough has rested, flour your work surface and roll out the dough into a 18- by 26-inch rectangle. Remember to keep flouring the work surface and moving the dough around so it does not stick to it.

Continued…

10. Spread the filling evenly over the dough, covering it completely. Starting from a long edge, roll the dough into a log. Cut the log into 1-inch slices. Place the slices, flat side down, in the skillet or baking dish, directly on top of the topping mixture.

11. Proof the buns until they double in size, about 1½ hours. Thirty minutes before they're done, preheat the oven to 350°F.

12. Bake the buns for 35 to 40 minutes or until golden brown.

13. Remove the buns from the oven. To serve, invert the skillet or baking dish over a platter or tray.

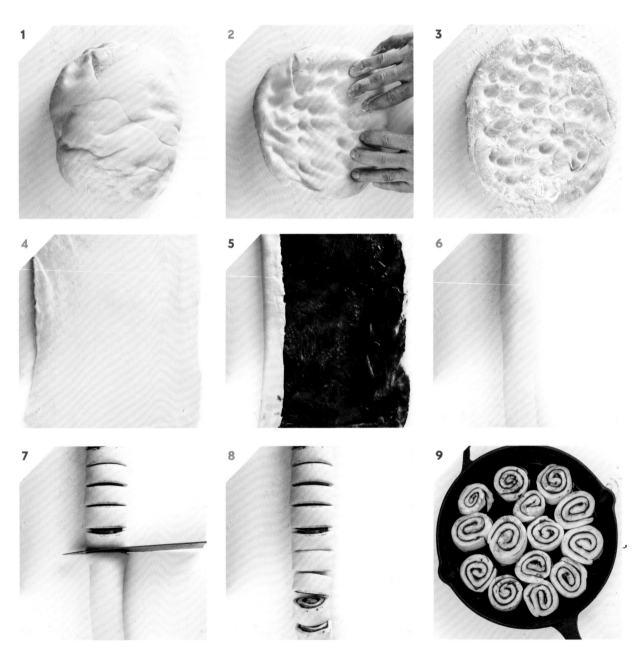

Milk Chocolate Cream–Filled Brioche Donuts

Makes 13 donuts
Prep Time: 2 hours
Cook Time: 15 minutes

Brioche Dough

1⅓ cups (200 g) bread flour

1⅓ cups (200 g) all-purpose flour

¼ cup (50 g) granulated sugar

2 teaspoons kosher salt

⅓ cup (75 ml) whole milk

2¼ teaspoons (7 g) active dry yeast

3 large eggs, room temperature

1 cup (225 g) unsalted butter,
    cut in cubes, room temperature

Milk Chocolate Cream

3 oz (80 g) milk chocolate

2 large eggs

¼ cup (50 g) granulated sugar

3 tablespoons (23 g) cornstarch

1 cup (250 ml) whole milk

¼ cup (60 ml) heavy cream

¼ cup (60 g) unsalted butter

Icing sugar, for dusting

Unlike traditional donuts that are fried, these brioche-style donuts are baked—but don't let that fool you into thinking they don't pack a punch. Brioche is a bread that is relatively high in fat, which makes these donuts rich, flavorful and tender. You can fill them with anything from jam to whipped cream. I've used a creamy milk chocolate pastry cream, which is like a custard.

1. For the brioche dough, combine the bread and all-purpose flours, sugar and salt in the bowl of a stand mixer fitted with the dough hook.

2. In a separate bowl, microwave the milk for 30 seconds, until just slightly warm, then add the yeast. Whisk together until the yeast dissolves, about 5 minutes. Whisk the eggs into the milk mixture, then transfer to the bowl of the stand mixer. Mix the dough on low speed until it comes together, about 5 minutes.

3. Once the dough has formed, slowly add the cubed butter, one-third at a time.

4. Increase the mixer speed to medium and mix for 10 to 15 minutes, until the butter is fully incorporated and the dough separates from the sides of the bowl and becomes shiny and smooth. If the dough still sticks to the bowl, mix for another 5 minutes.

5. Remove the dough from the bowl and knead by hand for 2 minutes. Place the dough in a greased bowl, cover and refrigerate until it becomes firm, about 15 minutes.

6. Meanwhile, make the milk chocolate cream. Roughly chop the milk chocolate and set it aside.

7. Whisk the eggs, sugar and cornstarch in a bowl; set aside.

8. Place the milk and cream in a medium pot and bring to a boil over high heat. Then set aside, off the heat. Pour one-quarter of the hot milk mixture into the egg mixture to temper the eggs, whisking vigorously until combined. Pour the tempered egg mixture into the pot, whisking to fully combine with the milk mixture. Cook on medium heat, whisking continuously, until the mixture becomes thick enough to coat the back of a spoon. Then add in the chopped milk chocolate, and mix until it has fully melted in. Immediately remove from the heat and strain into a clean bowl. Cool the mixture to room temperature; then use an immersion blender to mix in the butter, forming an emulsion.

Continued…

9. Cover the chocolate cream with plastic wrap, right against the surface, and place in the fridge until ready to use.

10. To make the donuts, portion the dough into 65-gram pieces, just a little bigger than a golf ball. Roll each piece into a tight, round ball and place the balls 2 inches apart on a baking sheet lined with parchment paper. Lightly cover with plastic wrap and proof until the dough balls double in size, 1 to 1½ hours.

11. Thirty minutes before the proofing is complete, preheat the oven to 350°F.

12. Bake the brioche donuts for 12 to 15 minutes, until lightly golden brown. Cool completely on a wire rack.

13. Once the donuts have cooled, fill a piping bag with the chocolate cream. Poke a hole in the side of each donut and fill with the cream. Dust the filled donut with icing sugar and serve.

NOTE

The chocolate cream can be made 1 day in advance, and it can be frozen for up to 1 month.

If you want a deep golden donut, brush an egg wash on the dough before baking (whisk together 1 whole egg and 1 tablespoon/15 ml milk or heavy cream).

Dark Chocolate Glazed Donuts

Makes 18 donuts

Prep Time: 15 minutes

Cook Time: 10 minutes

1²⁄₃ cups (250 g) all-purpose flour

¼ cup (30 g) Dutch-process cocoa powder

1¼ teaspoons baking powder

¼ teaspoon kosher salt

2 large eggs

½ cup + ⅓ cup (165 g) granulated sugar

½ cup (125 ml) whole milk

⅓ cup (75 ml) buttermilk

¼ cup (60 g) unsalted butter, melted

Glaze

3½ cups (440 g) icing sugar

½ cup (60 g) Dutch-process cocoa powder

²⁄₃ cup (150 ml) whole milk

Cake donuts are wonderful to make. They're moist and full of chocolate flavor, and they melt in your mouth. These donuts don't require a fryer; and because they're baked, they feel healthier. No yeast is used, so they're also quick and easy to make. You will need donut molds for this recipe.

1. Preheat the oven to 325°F.

2. Sift together the flour, cocoa powder, baking powder and salt into a bowl.

3. In a separate bowl, whisk the eggs, sugar, whole milk, buttermilk and melted butter until fully combined.

4. Pour the egg mixture into the flour mixture and mix until the batter just comes together. Don't overmix—the batter will be thick. Transfer the batter to a piping bag fitted with a plain round tip.

5. Pipe the batter into the donut molds until they are three-quarters full.

6. Bake the donuts for 10 minutes. Test, using a toothpick, to see if they are fully set in the middle. Once they are done, remove them immediately to a wire rack.

7. To make the glaze, sift together the icing sugar and cocoa powder into a bowl. Heat the milk in the microwave for 30 seconds. Whisk the warm milk into the sugar and cocoa mixture to fully incorporate.

8. Fully submerge each donut in the glaze mixture, then place on a wire rack set over a baking sheet lined with parchment paper to catch the excess as it drips off. Then enjoy! You can freeze any leftover glaze for future use.

NOTE

These donuts are best served the day you make them.

Double Chocolate Sour Cherry Muffins

Makes 24 muffins
Prep Time: 15 minutes
Cook Time: 28 minutes

1²/₃ cups (250 g) all-purpose flour

½ cup (60 g) Dutch-process cocoa powder

1 tablespoon (9 g) baking powder

¾ cup (150 g) granulated sugar

½ teaspoon kosher salt

3 large eggs

²/₃ cup + 2 teaspoons (160 ml) whole milk

6.7 oz (190 g) dark chocolate

¾ cup + 1 teaspoon (180 g) unsalted butter, melted

16 oz (450 g) frozen sour cherries, chopped (see Note)

When I think of classic pairings with chocolate, cherries are at the top of my list. These muffins are moist and rich. Any type of cherry or chocolate will work, but I love sour cherries with dark chocolate. The bitterness of the chocolate and the tartness of the cherries balance each other perfectly.

1. Preheat the oven to 350°F. Line two 12-cup muffin pans with paper liners.

2. In the bowl of a stand mixer fitted with the paddle attachment, combine the flour, cocoa powder, baking powder, sugar and salt.

3. In a separate bowl, whisk together the eggs and milk.

4. Chop the chocolate and place in a third bowl.

5. Add the egg mixture to the dry ingredients and mix on low speed until fully combined. Pour in the melted butter and mix to combine fully. Then fold in the chopped chocolate by hand, followed by the chopped cherries.

6. Pour equal portions of batter into the lined muffin pans, leaving ½ inch to the top of the liners.

7. Bake the muffins for 25 minutes or until a toothpick inserted in the center comes out clean.

8. Cool the muffins on a wire rack for 15 minutes, then remove from the pan. They can be frozen for up to 1 month or stored in the fridge for up to 1 week.

NOTE

When folding the cherries into the batter, make sure they are still frozen. This will ensure that they keep their shape and prevent the batter from becoming too wet.

White Chocolate Raspberry Scones

Makes 9 scones
Prep Time: 15 minutes
Cook Time: 18 to 20 minutes

1 cup (225 g) unsalted butter, cold

3½ cups + ⅓ cup (575 g)
  all-purpose flour

½ cup (100 g) granulated sugar

4 teaspoons (12 g) baking powder

1 teaspoon baking soda

1 teaspoon kosher salt

6.7 oz (190 g) white chocolate

1½ cups (375 ml) heavy cream

2 large eggs

1⅓ cups (200 g) frozen raspberries

1 tablespoon (8 g) icing sugar,
  optional

Egg Wash

1 large egg

2 tablespoons (30 ml) whole milk

Raspberries and white chocolate is one of my favorite pairings. The acidity of the berry stands up to the sweetness of the chocolate in a way that's just delicious. These scones are light and airy, with a beautiful outer crust for texture. If you'd rather try this recipe with a different berry, go for it, but if you're adding fresh berries, give them a quick freeze to firm up their structure, so they don't become mush when you fold them into the batter.

1. Preheat the oven to 325°F and line a baking sheet with parchment paper.

2. Cut the butter into 1-inch cubes and place on a plate in the freezer or fridge for about 10 minutes to get really cold.

3. In a bowl, combine the flour, sugar, baking powder, baking soda and salt.

4. Chop the white chocolate and set it aside.

5. In a separate bowl, whisk the cream and eggs to combine.

6. Using your hands, work the cold butter into the dry ingredients until it has the texture of coarse meal, being careful not to overmix.

7. Pour the cream mixture into the dry ingredients and gently stir together until just combined. Add the chopped chocolate and frozen raspberries and gently fold into the dough to distribute them evenly. If the dough is too wet, adjust the texture by dusting a little flour over the surface to achieve the right consistency. You should be able to move and pick up the dough without it sticking to your fingers or the work surface.

8. Flour your work surface and roll out the dough into a 9-inch square, adding a bit more flour if needed to keep it from sticking. Cut the square into 9 equal pieces. Place the pieces on the lined baking sheet and refrigerate for 10 minutes to chill the dough.

9. To make the egg wash, whisk together the egg and milk. Once the scones have chilled, lightly brush them with the egg wash, then bake for about 18 to 20 minutes, or until they're a light golden color. Before serving, you can dust the tops with icing sugar to add sweetness, if you like.

NOTE

The key to perfect scones is to start with cold butter and not overwork the dough. If the butter becomes warm as you work with it, place the flour-and-butter mixture in the fridge for 20 minutes, until it is cold again. Cold butter creates air pockets as the dough bakes, resulting in a flakier pastry.

Chocolate Zucchini Bread

Makes one 5- by 9-inch loaf
Prep Time: 15 minutes
Cook Time: 1 hour, 5 minutes

---

1 large (325 g) zucchini
2.5 oz (75 g) dark chocolate
2 cups (240 g) almond flour
⅓ cup (38 g) natural cocoa powder
1⅛ teaspoons baking soda
¾ teaspoon kosher salt
½ cup (150 g) honey
3 tablespoons (45 ml) coconut oil
1½ teaspoons vanilla extract
3 large eggs
1.8 oz (50 g) 70% semisweet
  chocolate chips

Chocolate zucchini bread takes me back to childhood memories of the garden harvest. This pairing really works. The zucchini has a subtle flavor but adds incredible moistness and texture to the loaf. The bitterness of the chocolate and the earthiness of the toasted almonds are cut slightly by the sugar and stand up nicely to the zucchini. Oh, and by the way, this chocolatey loaf is gluten-free and sweetened with honey.

1. Preheat the oven to 350°F and spray a 5- by 9-inch loaf pan with nonstick spray or line it with parchment paper.

2. Grate the zucchini in a food processor or using the largest holes of a box grater. Set aside in a strainer set over a bowl to drain off some of the liquid.

3. Chop the dark chocolate and set aside.

4. Mix the almond flour, cocoa powder, baking soda and salt in the bowl of a stand mixer fitted with the paddle attachment. Add the zucchini and mix to incorporate.

5. In a medium bowl, mix the honey, coconut oil and vanilla together. Microwave for about 30 seconds, until melted and lukewarm. Whisk in the eggs.

6. Pour the honey mixture into the dry ingredients and mix until the batter is fully blended. Fold in the chopped dark chocolate.

7. Transfer the batter to the prepared loaf pan and bake for about 1 hour and 5 minutes, or until a toothpick inserted in the center comes out clean.

8. Cool the loaf in the pan on a wire rack for 5 minutes. Then remove it from the pan and sprinkle the chocolate chips on top. The residual heat will partially melt them into the loaf. Once the loaf is fully cooled, you can wrap it in plastic wrap and store in the fridge, or freeze it for up to 1 month.

NOTE

The loaf becomes moister once chilled.

Sprinkling the chocolate chips on top of the loaf is optional, but it adds more texture. You can also dust the loaf with icing sugar to add sweetness.

Chocolate Babka

Makes one 10-inch loaf
Prep Time: 2½ hours
Cook Time: 60 to 65 minutes

Brioche Dough

1¼ cups (190 g) bread flour

1¼ cups (190 g) all-purpose flour

¼ cup (50 g) granulated sugar

2 teaspoons kosher salt

⅓ cup (75 ml) whole milk

1 teaspoon (7 g) active dry yeast

3 large eggs, room temperature

1 cup (225 g) unsalted butter, cold,
   cut into cubes

Filling

2.5 oz (75 g) dark chocolate,
   chopped

2 tablespoons + 2 teaspoons
   (40 g) unsalted butter,
   room temperature

⅓ cup (40 g) icing sugar

¼ cup (30 g) Dutch-process
   cocoa powder

Assembly

1.8 oz (50 g) semisweet chocolate,
   finely chopped

Egg Wash

1 large egg

1 tablespoon (15 ml) whole milk

I absolutely love this recipe. It's great for breakfast or an afternoon snack. Brioche is my favorite of all breads because it stays moist and is full of flavor. The chocolate filling here is rich and adds a little sweetness as it melts into the loaf. This babka is also awesome sliced and toasted, spread with lots of butter (I hope you're not scared of butter!).

1. For the brioche dough, combine the bread flour, all-purpose flour, sugar and salt in the bowl of a stand mixer fitted with the dough hook.

2. Warm the milk in the microwave for 30 seconds, until lukewarm. Add the yeast to the warm milk and whisk to dissolve. Let the mixture sit for 5 minutes; it will start to form bubbles as the yeast reacts. Add the eggs to the yeast mixture, mixing to combine.

3. Slowly pour the milk-and-egg mixture into the dry ingredients while mixing on low speed. Once all the ingredients have been mixed in and a dough has formed, add the butter, one cube at a time, to the mixing bowl. Increase the speed to medium and mix until the butter is fully incorporated and the dough is separating from the sides of the bowl, about 20 minutes. Clean the sides of the bowl once or twice as you mix. The dough should be smooth, shiny and elastic.

4. Remove the dough from the mixing bowl and place on a floured work surface. Give the dough 5 kneaded folds to bring it together. This develops the gluten structure of the dough and helps it to rise.

5. Place the dough on a floured baking sheet or in a lightly greased bowl. Lightly cover the top with plastic wrap and let it relax in the fridge for at least 45 minutes or up to 24 hours.

6. In the meantime, prepare the filling. Melt the chocolate in a double boiler (see page 7). Once it is melted, remove the bowl, add the butter and stir to combine until the butter has melted. Sift in the icing sugar and cocoa powder and stir to form a thick paste. Set the mixture aside and allow it to cool to room temperature.

7. Spray a 10-inch loaf pan with nonstick spray.

Continued…

8. Once the dough has rested, remove it from the fridge and roll it out into a 9- by 13-inch rectangle. Spread the filling evenly across the dough, leaving a ½-inch border on one long edge with no filling, so that when the dough is rolled up, it will stick together. Starting from the other long side, roll the dough into a log. Slice the log in half lengthwise, exposing the center of the roll. Create an X shape with the half-logs and then twist the ends around each other, keeping the filling face up. Tuck under the ends and place the dough in the prepared loaf pan. Cover with plastic wrap and set aside to proof in a warm area until the dough doubles in size, about 1½ hours.

9. Halfway through the proofing, preheat the oven to 325°F. Prepare the egg wash by whisking together the egg and milk.

10. When the dough has doubled in size, brush the top with the egg wash and bake in the oven for 60 to 65 minutes. You can check for doneness using a thermometer: stick it into the center of the loaf at its highest point—it should read between 190° and 200°F.

11. Remove the babka from the oven and set on a wire rack for 5 minutes, then remove it from the loaf pan. Serve warm, with your favorite chocolate hazelnut spread—and if you're interested in making your own, check out my Milk Chocolate Hazelnut Spread on page 243.

12. The babka can be placed in an airtight plastic bag and stored at room temperature for up to 5 days or in the fridge for up to 1 week. You can also freeze it for up to 2 months.

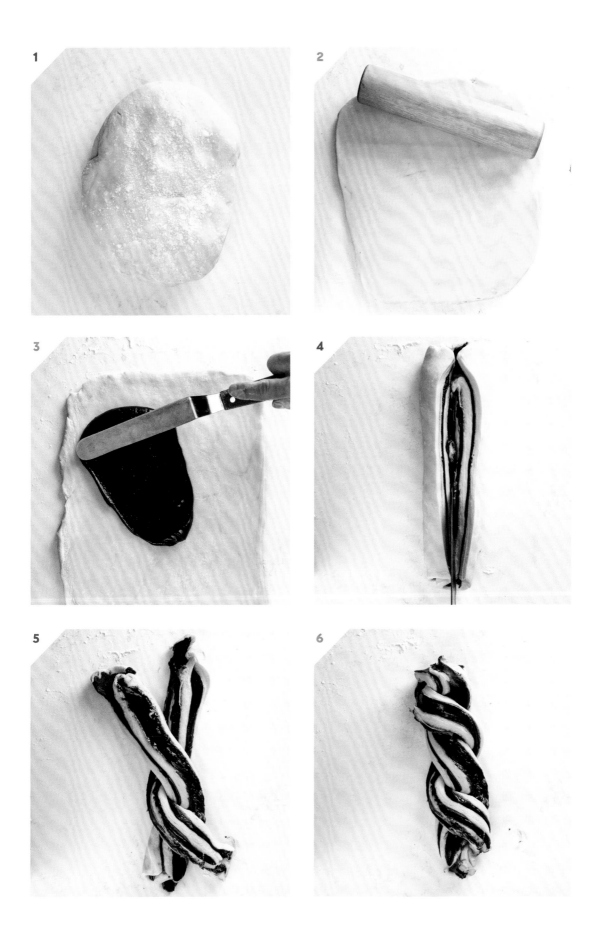

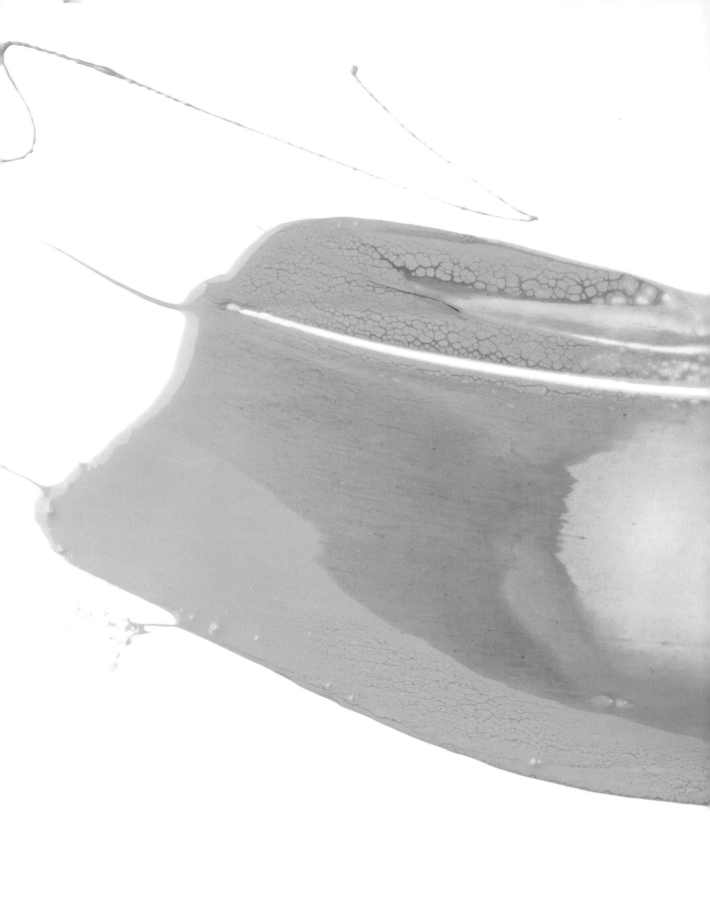

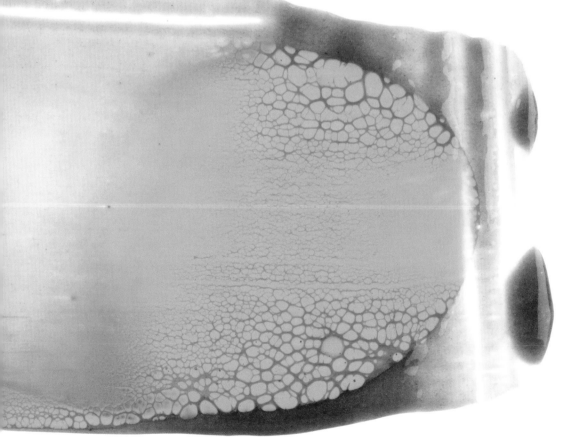

Cakes, Tarts & Soufflés

Flourless Chocolate Cake

Makes one 9-inch cake

Prep Time: 14 minutes

Cook Time: 15 to 20 minutes

---

10 oz (280 g) dark chocolate, chopped

½ cup (115 g) unsalted butter, room temperature

2 tablespoons + ¼ cup (75 g) granulated sugar, divided

5 large eggs, room temperature

Not only is this one of the easiest cakes to make, it's also gluten-free, which means just about everyone can enjoy it. I was first introduced to this cake by chef Gianni Picchi while working in an Italian restaurant early in my career. Gianni is retired now, but we still meet weekly for coffee at my pastry shop. This cake is full of chocolate flavor and is super moist. It's best served warm (not hot) with a dusting of icing sugar, but you can't go wrong if you add vanilla ice cream, crème anglaise (see page 240) or whipped cream instead. I'm guessing this cake is so easy to execute because we had to make it on the fly during restaurant service.

1. Preheat the oven to 325°F. Spray or line a 9-inch springform pan with parchment paper. Wrap the outside of the pan in aluminum foil in case of leakage.

2. Combine the chocolate, butter and 2 tablespoons of sugar in a bowl. Place the bowl over a simmering pot of water to create a double boiler and whisk to melt together and fully incorporate the ingredients. Remove from the heat and set aside.

3. Separate the eggs. In the bowl of a stand mixer fitted with the whisk attachment, whip the egg yolks to full volume, about 5 minutes, then transfer to a separate bowl. Clean and dry the mixing bowl, then whisk the egg whites and the remaining ¼ cup sugar to stiff peaks, about 5 minutes.

4. Fold the whipped egg yolks into the melted chocolate mixture. Then fold the egg whites into the mixture in thirds, being careful not to lose too much volume.

5. Pour the batter into the prepared pan and bake for 15 to 20 minutes. Once cooked, the top of the cake will form a crust and crack.

6. Remove the cake from the oven and let it cool in the pan. The cake will collapse, so don't worry that it's gone wrong! It's dense and fudgy but also delicate, so don't flip it over onto a wire rack. Once the cake has cooled, dust it with icing sugar and release the sides of the pan.

NOTE

You can substitute milk chocolate for the dark chocolate if you prefer.

Banana Cream Chocolate Pie

Makes one 9-inch pie

Prep Time: 55 minutes

Cook Time: 40 minutes

Brisée Dough

²/₃ cup (145 g) unsalted butter, cold

1 cup + 1 tablespoon (160 g) all-purpose flour

½ teaspoon kosher salt

3 tablespoons (45 ml) ice-cold water

Custard

1.5 oz (45 g) dark chocolate

1.5 oz (45 g) milk chocolate

4 large egg yolks

¼ cup (50 g) granulated sugar

3 tablespoons (23 g) cornstarch

1 cup + 2 tablespoons (280 ml) whole milk

¼ cup (60 g) unsalted butter, room temperature

½ cup (125 ml) mashed banana (about 1 large)

Bananas

4 large bananas, for layering

Whipped Cream

2 cups (500 ml) heavy cream

3 tablespoons (24 g) icing sugar

1 tablespoon (15 ml) vanilla extract

Shaved chocolate (see page 13), for garnish

For as long as I can remember, cream pies have been one of my favorite types. There's something special about the simplicity of flaky pie crust paired with a rich and creamy filling. Everyone has their favorite pie crust, but I love the flavor and texture of a pâte brisée, which is made with only butter as the fat (in other pie crusts you might see lard or shortening used). This is a light, fragile dough because of its high butter content. Unlike a short crust, it doesn't contain eggs.

1. For the brisée dough, cube the butter and place it in the freezer for about 10 minutes, or until very cold. Combine the flour and salt in a large bowl. Cut the cold butter into the dry ingredients with your fingers or a pastry blender until you achieve a coarse crumb. Sprinkle in the cold water and mix to form a dough (be careful not to overwork it). The dough can also be made in a food processor or a stand mixer fitted with the paddle attachment. Wrap the dough in plastic wrap and refrigerate for 1 hour, until it has relaxed and chilled.

2. While the dough is resting, chop the dark and milk chocolates for the custard and set aside in a bowl.

3. Whisk the egg yolks, sugar and cornstarch in a bowl and set aside.

4. Place the milk in a medium pot and bring to a boil over high heat. Remove the pot from the stove. Pour half of the hot milk into the egg mixture to temper it, whisking vigorously until combined. Then pour the tempered egg mixture into the pot of milk, whisking to combine fully. Cook the mixture over low heat, whisking continuously, until it becomes thick enough to coat the back of a spoon. Add the chopped chocolate and whisk until it has fully melted. Add the butter, then use an immersion blender to emulsify the butter and the custard mixture. Add the mashed banana and blend with the immersion blender until smooth.

5. Halfway through the dough resting time, preheat the oven to 350°F.

6. Once the dough is firm, take it out of the fridge and flour both sides. Flour your work surface and roll the dough into a circle about 12 inches in diameter and ¹/₈ inch thick. The dough circle should be a couple of inches bigger than the pie plate, because it will shrink during baking. Carefully transfer it to the pie dish, leaving a ¼-inch overhang, then trim off any excess dough. Line the dough with aluminum foil and add baking beans to weigh it down.

Continued…

7. Bake the pie crust for 15 minutes, then remove it from the oven. Remove the foil and baking beans. Place the crust back in the oven and bake for another 10 minutes, until a light golden brown. Allow the crust to cool. If the dough puffs up, press it down with your fingers.

8. Once the pie crust has cooled, it's time to start layering. Cut 3 bananas into slices about ¼ inch thick. Cover the entire bottom of the pie shell with banana slices. Then add half of the custard, to halfway up the sides. Repeat with the remaining sliced bananas and custard.

9. For the whipped cream, combine the cream, icing sugar and vanilla in a bowl. Beat with an electric mixer at medium speed until medium peaks form, about 5 minutes.

10. Top the pie with the whipped cream and the remaining banana, sliced ¼ inch thick. Garnish with shaved chocolate. Place in the fridge for 1 hour to set. The pie will last in the fridge for up to 3 days.

NOTE

This pie is best served cold, straight from the fridge, to maintain its structure.

Dark Chocolate Passionfruit Tart

Makes one 9-inch tart
Prep Time: 15 minutes
Cook Time: 1 hour, 10 minutes

Tart Shell

½ cup (115 g) unsalted butter, room temperature

½ cup (65 g) icing sugar

¼ teaspoon kosher salt

1 large egg, room temperature

1½ cups (225 g) all-purpose flour

2 tablespoons (15 g) almond flour

2 tablespoons (15 g) Dutch-process cocoa powder

Passionfruit Filling

4 large eggs

½ cup (125 ml) heavy cream

⅓ cup (75 ml) passionfruit purée

¼ cup (50 g) granulated sugar

White chocolate curls (see page 13), for garnish

I love to incorporate tropical fruits into my desserts, especially passionfruit. Passionfruit and chocolate share similar citrus and floral notes, making them a perfect pairing. I use the chocolate tart shell for its rich structural texture and the creamy passionfruit filling for balance. It adds a delicious bite of acidity and bitterness.

1. Preheat the oven to 325°F.

2. For the tart shell, combine the butter, icing sugar and salt in the bowl of a stand mixer fitted with the paddle attachment. Cream until light and fluffy. Add the egg and beat to combine, until fluffy.

3. Sift together the all-purpose flour, almond flour and cocoa powder. Add to the butter mixture, beating on medium-low speed until it just comes together. Remove the dough from the bowl, flatten into a square and wrap with plastic wrap. Chill in the fridge for 20 minutes.

4. While the dough is resting, make the passionfruit filling. Combine the eggs, cream, passionfruit purée and sugar in a bowl and blend with an immersion blender. Strain the mixture into a clean bowl and set aside.

5. Remove the dough from the fridge and lightly flour your work surface. Roll out the dough to 12 inches in diameter and about ⅛ inch thick.

6. Spray a tart pan with nonstick spray, then line it with the dough, letting it hang over the sides without stretching it. Trim off any excess.

7. Line the bottom of the tart shell with aluminum foil and fill with baking beans. Bake in the preheated oven for 10 minutes. Remove the baking beans and bake for another 5 minutes, until light golden brown. Remove from the oven and let cool completely.

8. Reduce the oven temperature to 210°F. Fill the tart shell to the top with the passionfruit filling. Place in the oven and bake for 45 to 50 minutes, or until the center is set and not jiggly.

9. Remove from the oven and place in the fridge to cool. Once the tart is cool, remove the pan.

NOTE

The tart can be frozen for up to 1 month or left in the fridge for 2 days, until the shell becomes soft.

White Chocolate Passionfruit Mousse Cake

Makes one 8-inch square cake
Prep Time: 1 hour, plus 2 hours, 30 minutes for freezing
Cook Time: 1 hour, 30 minutes

Almond Joconde

3 large eggs

1 cup (120 g) ground almonds

¾ cup (100 g) icing sugar

¼ cup (37 g) all-purpose flour

4 large egg whites

2½ tablespoons (30 g) granulated sugar

2 tablespoons (30 g) unsalted butter, melted

Passionfruit Crémeux

2 gelatin sheets or ½ tablespoon (4 g) gelatin powder

1 cup (250 ml) passionfruit purée

7 large egg yolks

3 large eggs

¾ cup (150 g) granulated sugar

½ cup + 1 tablespoon (130 g) unsalted butter, melted

White Chocolate Topper

1½ gelatin sheets or ⅜ tablespoon (3 g) gelatin powder

¼ cup (60 ml) passionfruit purée

¼ cup (60 ml) whole milk

2¼ teaspoons (15 g) corn syrup

2.5 oz (70 g) white chocolate, chopped

¼ cup (60 ml) heavy cream, cold

Continued…

Passionfruit pairs well with dark, milk or white chocolate. I love this combination of white chocolate and passionfruit because the sweetness of the chocolate plays well with the acidity of the fruit. They balance each other to create a refreshingly light dessert. The style of the passionfruit cream is called a *crémeux*, meaning creamy. It's soft and melts in the mouth. For the cake, I use a classic joconde sponge, which is a light and airy French sponge with a nutty presence.

1. Preheat the oven to 325°F. Line a 13- by 18-inch baking sheet with parchment paper.

2. For the joconde sponge, place the eggs, ground almonds and icing sugar in the bowl of a stand mixer fitted with the paddle attachment. Whip to combine, about 5 minutes. Transfer to a separate bowl.

3. Sift the flour and set it aside.

4. Place the egg whites in the cleaned, dry bowl of the stand mixer fitted with the whisk attachment, and whip until they become frothy. Add the sugar and whip to stiff peaks.

5. Mix the flour into the egg-and-almond mixture to fully combine. Fold in the egg whites in 3 additions, being careful not to take out too much air. Fold in the melted butter, just until combined.

6. Spread the batter on the lined baking sheet and bake for 8 to 10 minutes. Remove from the oven and let cool. Cut out an 8-inch square piece from the sponge and place it in an 8-inch square cake frame, set on a baking sheet lined with parchment paper. This is the beginning stage of building the cake.

7. For the crémeux, bloom the gelatin in cold water until fully hydrated, about 5 minutes. Once it's hydrated, remove the sheets and squeeze out the excess water. If using powdered gelatin, the ratio is 5 parts water to 1 part gelatin.

8. Prepare an ice bath and set it aside.

9. In a bowl, combine the passionfruit purée, egg yolks, whole eggs and sugar. Place the bowl over a pot of simmering water. Cook the mixture to 180°F, whisking constantly. Remove the bowl from the double boiler and whisk in the bloomed gelatin to dissolve.

10. Place the bowl over the ice bath to cool it quickly. Add the butter and use an immersion blender to emulsify the mixture. Make sure all the butter is fully incorporated to create a smooth texture.

Continued…

White Chocolate Mousse

2 gelatin sheets or ½ tablespoon
    (4 g) gelatin powder

1 cup (250 ml) heavy cream

2 large egg yolks

¼ cup (50 g) granulated sugar

½ cup (125 ml) whole milk

3.5 oz (100 g) white chocolate

11. Pour the crémeux over the sponge in the cake frame. Place the sheet with the frame in the fridge for 30 minutes to set.

12. For the white chocolate topper, bloom the gelatin in cold water. Once it's hydrated, strain and squeeze out the remaining water.

13. In a pot set over medium heat, combine the passionfruit purée, milk and corn syrup. Bring to a boil, then dissolve the bloomed gelatin in the hot liquid.

14. Strain the mixture over the chopped white chocolate and emulsify with an immersion blender to create a smooth, shiny consistency. Pour in the cold cream and whisk to combine. Transfer to a container and place in the fridge until the assembly stage.

15. For the white chocolate mousse, bloom the gelatin in cold water. Once it's hydrated, strain and squeeze out the remaining water.

16. Whisk the cream to medium peaks and place in the fridge to keep cold until needed.

17. In a separate bowl, whisk together the egg yolks and sugar.

18. Place the milk in a small pot and bring to a boil over medium heat. Once boiling, pour half of the milk into the egg yolk mixture to temper the eggs, then pour the mixture into the pot with the remaining milk. Return the pot to low heat and whisk until the mixture reaches 180°F or is thick enough to coat the back of a spoon. Remove the pot from the heat and stir in the bloomed gelatin, until dissolved.

19. Cool the mixture over an ice bath until the mixture is cold. Fold in the whipped cream.

20. Take the sheet with the cake frame out of the fridge. Pour the mousse over the crémeux layer and spread it evenly across the surface. Place in the freezer for about 30 minutes to set, then pour the white chocolate topper evenly across the mousse. Set in the freezer for 2 hours.

21. Once the mousse is frozen, remove the cake from the frame. You can do this by soaking a knife in warm water and running it along the inside edge of the frame, or you can use a kitchen torch to heat the sides of the frame so it slides off easily.

22. To serve, slice the cake with a knife dipped in hot water for even and clean cuts. Keep the cake in the fridge until ready to eat.

NOTE

To give the top of the cake a nice shine, boil together equal parts water and apricot jam. Spread over the top of the cake with a pastry brush before serving.

Mango Caramel Mousse Cake

Makes one 8-inch square or round cake

Prep Time: 1 hour, plus 3 hours for freezing

Cook Time: 25 minutes

Chocolate Sponge

13.2 oz (375 oz) 70% dark chocolate

¼ cup (60 g) unsalted butter

10 large eggs, separated, room temperature

½ cup + ⅓ cup (165 g) granulated sugar

Chocolate Sheet

3.5 oz (100 g) dark chocolate

Mango Crémeux

2 gelatin sheets or ½ tablespoon (4 g) gelatin powder

1 cup (250 ml) mango purée

7 large egg yolks

3 large eggs

¾ cup (150 g) granulated sugar

½ cup + 1 tablespoon (130 g) unsalted butter

Milk Chocolate Caramel Mousse

⅔ cup + 2¼ cups (720 ml) heavy cream, divided

½ cup (100 g) granulated sugar

4 large egg yolks, whisked

11 oz (320 g) milk chocolate, chopped

5 gelatin sheets or 1 tablespoon (8 g) gelatin powder

Dark Chocolate Glaze (page 43)

Chocolate swirls (see page 15), for garnish

If you're looking for a statement dessert with an explosion of flavor, this gluten-free cake is just the ticket. This dessert will push you to become a more elevated baker. It is difficult to produce, but it's so rewarding, I think you should give it a try. It's rich, creamy and, with the bold notes of tropical fruits, fresh. Everyone always asks for seconds!

1. Preheat the oven to 325°F. Line a 13- by 18-inch baking sheet with parchment paper.

2. For the chocolate sponge, chop the chocolate and place in a bowl with the butter. Place the bowl over a simmering pot of water to create a double boiler and melt the mixture. Remove from the pot and set aside.

3. Place the egg whites in the bowl of a stand mixer fitted with the whisk attachment and whisk until they become frothy. Slowly add the sugar and continue whisking until stiff peaks form.

4. Whisk the egg yolks into the chocolate mixture to combine. Fold in the egg whites in 3 additions, being careful not to remove too much air. Spread the batter on the lined baking sheet and bake in the oven for 12 minutes. Remove from the oven and let cool completely.

5. Prepare the chocolate sheet by following the tempering instructions on page 8. Once it is tempered, spread the chocolate evenly across a sheet of acetate or waxed paper. Allow the chocolate to partially set—the chocolate should be soft to touch but not stick to your finger, and you should be able to score it without cracking. Using a ruler to measure, cut out an 8-inch square. Place a piece of acetate on top of the square and place a baking sheet over that to help it set flat. Leave the sheet on top until ready to use the chocolate sheet.

6. Cut an 8-inch square out of the chocolate sponge and place it in an 8-inch square cake frame. Set aside.

7. For the mango crémeux, bloom the gelatin sheets in cold water until fully hydrated, about 5 minutes. Remove the sheets and squeeze out any remaining water. For powdered gelatin, use 4 teaspoons (20 ml) cold water to bloom it (the ratio is 5 parts water to 1 part powdered gelatin).

8. Prepare an ice bath and set it aside.

9. In a bowl, whisk together the mango purée, egg yolks, whole eggs and sugar. Place the bowl over a pot of simmering water and cook the mixture to 180°F, whisking continuously so the egg does not scramble. The mixture will thicken enough to coat the back of a spoon.

Continued…

10. Remove the bowl from the pot, add the bloomed gelatin and whisk to fully dissolve the gelatin. Place the pot in the ice bath to cool the mixture until cold.

11. Add the butter to the chilled mixture. Emulsify using an immersion blender to create a smooth texture.

12. Pour the mango crémeux over the sponge in the cake frame. Then remove the acetate from the chocolate square, place the square over the crémeux and press gently to help it adhere.

13. For the mousse, place the $^2/_3$ cup of cream in a pot and bring to a boil over medium heat. Set aside.

14. In a separate pot, use the sugar to make a dry caramel. Place the pot on medium heat to warm it up, then reduce the heat to low. Sprinkle in one-quarter of the sugar and heat until the sugar liquefies. Add the rest of the sugar and slowly stir until it turns a light golden color. Immediately remove from the heat and, whisking constantly, slowly pour in the hot cream. Reduce the heat to low, return the caramel to the heat, and cook for 1 minute.

15. Remove the pot from the heat and pour half of the caramel cream into the egg yolks, whisking to combine. Then add the egg yolk mixture to the pot with the caramel cream. Return the pot to low heat and cook, whisking continuously, until it reaches 180°F or is thick enough to coat the back of a spoon.

16. Place the chopped chocolate in a bowl. Strain the caramel-egg mixture over the chocolate. Whisk to fully combine and melt, then immediately place the bowl in the ice bath to cool the caramel cream.

17. While the caramel cream is cooling, whisk the remaining 2¼ cups cream to medium peaks. Fold it into the cooled caramel cream.

18. Pour the mousse into the frame over the chocolate sheet. Place the cake in the freezer to set for 3 hours.

19. Once it is set, remove the cake from the freezer and remove the frame. You can do this by soaking a knife in warm water and running it around the inside edge of the frame, or you can use a kitchen torch to heat the sides of the frame so it slides off easily.

20. Cover the top of the cake with the dark chocolate glaze. To serve, cut the cake into equal squares and garnish with chocolate swirls.

Pineapple Chocolate Pavlova

Makes five 5-ounce portions
Prep Time: 20 minutes
Cook Time: 3 hours, 20 minutes

---

1 pineapple

Swiss Meringue
7 large egg whites
2 cups (400 g) granulated sugar
3 oz (85 g) dark chocolate

Whipped Cream
1 cup (250 ml) heavy cream
2 tablespoons (16 g) icing sugar
Dark chocolate shavings
 (see page 13), for garnish

Nothing tells your taste buds it's summer quite like a properly prepared pavlova. This dessert is a staple in our household and our pastry shop all summer long. The meringue in a pavlova should be crisp and dry on the outside but soft in the middle. It's delicious served with fresh fruit and berries of the season, along with a dollop of whipped cream.

1. Preheat the oven to 375°F. Line a baking sheet with parchment paper.

2. Peel and core the pineapple, then cut into 1-inch pieces or cubes. Roast on the lined baking sheet for 20 minutes. Set aside to cool at room temperature.

3. Lower the oven temperature to 180°F.

4. To make the Swiss meringue, combine the egg whites and sugar in a bowl, whisking well. Place the bowl over a pot of simmering water to create a double boiler, and whisk until the sugar has fully dissolved and the mixture becomes translucent.

5. Transfer the egg whites to the bowl of a stand mixer fitted with the whisk attachment. Mix until they reach stiff peaks. While the egg whites are mixing, chop the chocolate and melt it in the microwave in 30-second increments (see page 7).

6. Lightly fold the melted chocolate into the egg-white meringue.

7. Line a large baking sheet with parchment paper. Using a 5-ounce ice-cream scoop, place 5 portions of meringue on the sheet (you may need to do this in batches). Dip a spoon in hot water and make an indentation in the middle of each portion.

8. Bake the meringues for 2 hours, then turn off the oven and leave them there for 1 additional hour.

9. For the whipped cream, whisk together the cream and icing sugar to medium peaks. Place in the fridge until needed for assembly.

10. To assemble, place one meringue on a plate, dollop some whipped cream into the indentation and add the roasted pineapple. Garnish with chocolate shavings and serve.

NOTE

Roasting pineapple gives it a sweet, candy-like taste. You can also use fresh pineapple.

To store the meringues, tightly wrap them in plastic wrap, put them in an airtight container and store in a cool, dry place for up to 1 month.

Whipped Mascarpone White Chocolate Strawberry Cheesecake

Makes one 8-inch round cake
Prep Time: 2 hours, 20 minutes
Cook Time: 10 minutes

Graham Crumb Base

1¼ cups (150 g) graham cracker crumbs

2 tablespoons (25 g) granulated sugar

¼ cup (60 g) unsalted butter, melted

Cheesecake

4 gelatin sheets or 1 tablespoon (8 g) gelatin powder

2 cups (500 ml) heavy cream, divided

1 cup + 2 tablespoons (280 ml) strawberry purée

5 tablespoons (60 g) granulated sugar

2 cups (450 g) mascarpone cheese

6.7 oz (190 g) white chocolate, chopped

Sliced strawberries, for garnish

NOTE

You can use different fruit purées.

The cheesecake can be frozen for up to 2 months.

Mascarpone is like a combination of cream cheese, ricotta and crème fraîche, although a bit sweeter and more acidic. It pairs extremely well with white chocolate, and strawberries enhance the sweetness. This dessert is a fresh taste of summer on a plate.

1. Preheat the oven to 325°F. Line an 8-inch round springform pan with parchment paper.

2. Combine the graham cracker crumbs and sugar in a bowl.

3. Melt the butter in the microwave in 30-second increments, then pour it into the graham cracker mixture and combine well.

4. Pour the mixture into the lined pan and evenly press down the graham crumbs, using a glass with a flat bottom. Bake in the preheated oven for 10 minutes, then remove it from the oven and let cool completely.

5. For the cheesecake, bloom the gelatin sheets in cold water until fully hydrated, about 5 minutes. Remove the sheets and squeeze out the excess water. If using powdered gelatin, the ratio is 5 parts water to 1 part powdered gelatin.

6. In the bowl of a stand mixer fitted with the whisk attachment, beat 1 cup of heavy cream on medium speed until it reaches soft peaks. Set aside in a separate bowl in the fridge.

7. In a small pot over medium heat, heat the strawberry purée, sugar and remaining 1 cup cream. Add the bloomed gelatin to the strawberry mixture. Stir to combine and fully melt the gelatin. Strain the mixture into a clean bowl and set the bowl in an ice bath to cool to room temperature.

8. In the bowl of the stand mixer fitted with the paddle attachment, whip the mascarpone cheese until smooth. Slowly add the cooled strawberry mixture on low speed and mix until fully combined. Fold in the whipped cream, incorporating it fully.

9. Pour the cheesecake mixture into the graham crumb crust and spread it out evenly.

10. Place the cheesecake in the fridge for 2 hours to set or in the freezer for 1 hour. To serve, remove from the pan and garnish with sliced fresh strawberries.

White Chocolate Raspberry Parfaits

Makes four 6-ounce parfaits
Prep Time: 1 hour
Cook Time: 8 minutes

Crunchy Streusel

½ cup (85 g) all-purpose flour

¼ cup (55 g) brown sugar

¼ cup (50 g) granulated sugar

Pinch kosher salt

¼ cup (60 g) unsalted butter, room temperature

Raspberry Mousse

2 gelatin sheets or ½ tablespoon (4 g) gelatin powder

⅔ cup + 1 teaspoon (155 ml) whole milk

1½ teaspoons corn syrup

½ cup (125 ml) raspberry purée

10.3 oz (290 g) white chocolate

½ cup + ⅓ cup (205 ml) heavy cream, cold

White Chocolate Mousse

2 gelatin sheets or ½ tablespoon (4 g) gelatin powder

5 oz (140 g) white couverture chocolate

1 cup (250 ml) heavy cream

2 large egg yolks

2 tablespoons (26 g) granulated sugar, divided

2 large egg whites

Fresh raspberries, for garnish

Chocolate shavings (see page 13), for garnish

Parfait desserts are simple, elegant and easy to execute, especially if you have leftover mousse and sponge cake. Just throw them into a serving glass and you have a tasty new dessert. Raspberries are one of my favorite berries. They pair perfectly with milk, dark or white chocolate, but just about any fruit will work well in a parfait.

1. Preheat the oven to 325°F. Line a 13- by 18-inch baking sheet with parchment paper.

2. For the streusel, combine the flour, brown sugar, granulated sugar and salt in a bowl. Cut in the butter, using your fingers to create a fine texture.

3. Spread the streusel mixture on the lined baking sheet and bake for about 8 minutes, until golden brown. Remove from the oven and let cool completely. Store in an airtight container at room temperature.

4. For the raspberry mousse, bloom the gelatin sheets in cold water until fully hydrated, about 5 minutes. Remove the sheets and squeeze out any excess water. If using powdered gelatin, the ratio is 5 parts water to 1 part powdered gelatin.

5. In a pot, combine the milk, corn syrup and raspberry purée. Place on the stove and bring to a simmer. Remove from the heat, add the bloomed gelatin and stir to melt it in. Strain the mixture over the white chocolate in a bowl; emulsify with an immersion blender until fully combined.

6. Transfer the mixture to a plastic measuring jug that has enough room to add the cream, and pour in the cold cream. Mix to combine and place in the fridge to set for about 30 minutes.

7. For the white chocolate mousse, prepare the gelatin as in Step 4 above.

8. Place the white chocolate in a heatproof bowl and melt in the microwave in 30-second increments (see page 7). Set aside.

9. Whip the cream to medium peaks and set aside.

10. Combine the egg yolks and 1 tablespoon of sugar in a bowl. Place the bowl over a pot of simmering water to create a double boiler. Whisk the yolks and sugar until the mixture reaches 180°F—you are making a sabayon. Then add the bloomed gelatin and whisk to melt it in.

Continued…

11. Remove the bowl from the double boiler and immediately fold one-third of the whipped cream into the mixture. Then fold that mixture into the melted chocolate. Fold the remaining whipped cream into the chocolate mixture and set aside.

12. Make a meringue by placing the egg whites in the bowl of a stand mixer fitted with the whisk attachment, or use a hand mixer. Whisk the egg whites until frothy, then slowly add the remaining 1 tablespoon sugar and whisk until it reaches stiff peaks. Fold the meringue into the chocolate mixture to fully combine.

13. To assemble, spoon raspberry mousse into a parfait glass to about one-quarter of the way up. Add the white chocolate mousse to halfway up, and then fill the rest of the glass with more raspberry mousse. Garnish the top with streusel and fresh raspberries.

Black Forest Parfaits

Makes 4 martini-glass servings
Prep Time: 45 minutes
Cook Time: 10 to 12 minutes

Chocolate Sponge

11 large egg whites

¾ cup (150 g) granulated sugar

⅓ cup + 1 teaspoon (80 g)
 unsalted butter

9.2 oz (260 g) dark chocolate

4 large egg yolks

Cherry Compote

¼ cup (50 g) granulated sugar

½ teaspoon pectin

¼ cup (60 ml) water

3 cups (500 g) whole pitted
 sweet cherries

Vanilla Cream Mousse

5 gelatin sheets or 1 tablespoon
 (10 g) gelatin powder

2½ cups (625 ml) heavy cream,
 divided

½ cup (125 ml) whole milk

1 vanilla bean or 1 tablespoon (15 ml)
 vanilla extract

6 large egg yolks

⅓ cup (73 g) granulated sugar

Chocolate Mousse

½ cup + ⅓ cup (205 ml) heavy
 cream

4.4 oz (125 g) dark chocolate

⅓ cup + 2 tablespoons (110 ml)
 whole milk

Chocolate shavings (see page 13),
 for garnish

The first cake I learned to make as a young chef in culinary school was a Black Forest cake. It was also the cake that always stood out for me in bakery cases when I went shopping with my mom. This is Black Forest cake with a delicious twist. I've given it more flavor, color and texture by swapping out the whipped cream for two styles of mousse. I also use fresh sweet cherries, which adds a luscious brightness.

1. Preheat the oven to 350°F. Line a 13- by 18-inch baking sheet with parchment paper.

2. For the sponge, place the egg whites in the bowl of a stand mixer fitted with the whisk attachment, and beat until frothy. Then slowly stream in the sugar and whisk until stiff peaks are achieved.

3. Melt the butter and chocolate together in the microwave in 30-second increments. Whisk in the egg yolks.

4. Fold the egg whites into the chocolate mixture in 3 additions, making sure not to remove too much air.

5. Spread the batter on the lined baking sheet and bake for 10 to 12 minutes. Let the sponge cool completely at room temperature.

6. For the cherry compote, combine the sugar, and pectin in a pot, whisking to incorporate completely. Add the water and bring to a boil. Add the cherries and simmer on low heat for 10 minutes, until the liquid thickens. Remove from the heat and pour onto a rimmed baking sheet to cool.

7. For the vanilla mousse, bloom the gelatin sheets in cold water until fully hydrated, about 5 minutes. Remove the sheets and squeeze out the excess water. If using powdered gelatin, the ratio is 5 parts water to 1 part powdered gelatin.

8. In the bowl of a stand mixer fitted with the whisk attachment, or by hand, whisk 2 cups of cream to medium peaks.

9. Combine the milk, remaining ½ cup cream and vanilla in a pot and bring to a boil. Set aside.

10. Prepare an ice bath and set it aside.

11. Whisk together the egg yolks and sugar. Temper the egg yolks with half of the warm milk mixture, whisking constantly. Pour the tempered yolks into the pot with the remaining milk mixture, and cook on low heat until the mixture is thick enough to coat the back of a spoon.

12. Once the custard has thickened, immediately add the bloomed gelatin and whisk until fully dissolved. Strain the mixture into a separate bowl and place it in the ice bath to cool quickly.

Continued…

13. Fold the whipped cream into the cooled custard.

14. For the chocolate mousse, use a hand mixer or whisk to whip the cream to soft peaks.

15. Melt the chocolate in the microwave in 30-second increments, then set aside.

16. Place the milk in a small pot and bring to a boil. Once boiling, pour it over the melted chocolate and whisk to emulsify and create a smooth consistency. Fold the whipped cream into the chocolate mixture.

17. To assemble, cut the chocolate sponge into 8 pieces that are the same diameter as the serving glasses.

18. Place a spoonful of cherry compote in the bottom of each glass, followed by a piece of chocolate sponge. Then add 1 inch of the vanilla cream mousse, followed by a second piece of sponge. Almost fill the glass with the chocolate mousse, followed by more cherry compote. Garnish with chocolate shavings.

NOTE

Store the parfaits in the fridge, but allow them to sit at room temperature for 30 minutes before serving.

Chocolate Soufflés

Makes four 5-ounce servings
Prep Time: 18 minutes
Cook Time: 15 minutes

Ramekin Preparation

1 tablespoon (15 g) unsalted butter, room temperature

2 tablespoons (25 g) granulated sugar

Soufflés

4 large eggs, separated

½ teaspoon lemon juice

2 tablespoons (25 g) granulated sugar

5.6 oz (160 g) dark chocolate, chopped

¼ cup (60 g) unsalted butter, room temperature

1 teaspoon vanilla extract

⅛ teaspoon kosher salt

Icing sugar, for dusting

NOTE

These soufflés are best served with crème anglaise—try my White Chocolate Crème Anglaise on page 240.

The soufflé is a classic French dessert whose name literally translates to "breath" or "explosion." That makes sense, because this dessert really does behave like a deep breath or an explosion, rising to great heights if it's made correctly. It is an egg-based dish that is soft and fluffy on the inside and can accommodate all kinds of flavors, from sweet to savory. In my early restaurant career, soufflés were a popular standard on any menu. It's a simple dish, but there are a few important techniques to follow. I'm here to help you handle this recipe like a pro.

1. Preheat the oven to 375°F.

2. First, prepare 4 ramekin dishes. Using a pastry brush, coat the insides of the ramekins with the soft butter. Make the brush strokes from the bottom of the ramekin to the top—in the direction that the soufflé will rise. Fill one ramekin with sugar to the rim, then empty the sugar into the next ramekin, repeating until all 4 have been coated.

3. Next, separate the eggs. Place the whites in a bowl along with the lemon juice. Place the yolks in a separate bowl.

4. Using a hand mixer or a stand mixer fitted with the whisk attachment, whip the egg whites to soft peaks. Lightly sprinkle in the sugar and continue whipping until they form stiff peaks.

5. In a microwave-safe bowl, combine the chocolate and butter. Melt in the microwave in 30-second increments, stirring to combine fully.

6. Add the melted chocolate and butter to the egg yolks, along with the vanilla extract. Whisk together to create a paste.

7. Add one-third of the egg whites to the chocolate mixture and mix to lighten the paste. Then add the rest of the whites, folding very gently to fully incorporate the mixture while retaining as much air in the egg whites as possible.

8. Spoon the mixture into the ramekins to just above the rim. Take an offset spatula to each ramekin and level the mixture to the top of the ramekin.

9. Run your index finger around the inside rim of each dish to create a clean trench. This will ensure that the batter does not stick to the sides of the ramekin as it bakes.

10. Put the ramekins on a baking sheet and place in the preheated oven. Bake for about 15 minutes, or until the soufflés have risen.

11. Carefully remove the soufflés from the oven. Don't bang or slam the baking sheet and deflate them!

12. Dust with icing sugar and serve immediately.

Creamy Chocolate Mousse Cups

Makes 4 servings
Prep Time: 10 minutes

---

3 cups (750 ml) heavy cream
9 oz (250 g) milk chocolate
9 oz (250 g) dark chocolate
Fresh fruit, for garnish
Chocolate shavings (see page 13), for garnish

This is the perfect quick and easy mousse for any dinner party. Cream acts as the stabilizer, and the parfait cup supports the mousse without any gelatin necessary. It's light, airy and—most important when you're putting together a complicated dinner menu—very easy to make. This mousse can be made with any type of chocolate. And not only can you enjoy it on its own, it's great as a cake filling or served with fresh fruit and cookie crumbs or chopped chocolate for crunch.

1. Whisk the cream to soft peaks and set aside.

2. Chop the milk and dark chocolate. Heat together in the microwave in 20-second increments until fully melted (see page 7).

3. Whisk one-third of the whipped cream into the melted chocolate. Then mix in another one-third of the cream until fully combined. Fold in the rest of the cream very gently—you want to retain as much volume as possible.

4. Spoon or pipe the mousse into parfait cups, garnish with fresh fruit and chocolate shavings and serve at room temperature.

NOTE
The cream must be whisked just to soft peaks, because when you add it to the chocolate, it will stiffen up—you don't want it to get tough.

Chocolate Tres Leches

Makes one 9- by 13-inch cake

Prep Time: 35 minutes

Cook Time: 1 hour

Chocolate Chiffon Cake

½ cup + ⅓ cup (205 ml) water

¾ cup (90 g) Dutch-process
   cocoa powder

½ cup + 2 teaspoons (135 ml)
   canola oil

7 large eggs, separated, + 1 large
   egg white

1 cup (200 g) granulated sugar

1 teaspoon vanilla extract

2½ cups (325 g) pastry or cake flour

1 teaspoon kosher salt

2¼ tablespoons (20 g) baking
   powder

1 cup (130 g) icing sugar, sifted

Milk Mixture

12 oz (354 ml) can evaporated milk

14 oz (414 ml) can condensed milk

¼ cup (60 ml) chocolate milk
   (page 223)

Topping

2 cups (500 ml) heavy cream

3 tablespoons (24 g) icing sugar

1 tablespoon (8 g) Dutch-process
   cocoa powder

Grated dark chocolate
   or chocolate shavings
   (see page 13), for garnish

NOTE

*This cake is best left in the fridge
for a day before eating, to allow it
to absorb all the milk.*

This is what I like to call the moistest cake you'll ever try. Tres leches, or 3 milks cake, originated in Latin America. The first time I made it, I was a chef apprentice at a place called Portos Bakery in Glendale, California, and it's been a part of my repertoire ever since. There's nothing fancy about this cake; in fact, it's better served without much fuss, because it simply speaks for itself. I am confident this will become one of your favorites too.

1. Preheat the oven to 350°F.

2. For the chocolate chiffon cake, bring the water to a boil in a pot. Once boiling, whisk in the cocoa powder. Set aside, off the heat, to cool.

3. In a large bowl, combine the oil, egg yolks, granulated sugar and vanilla. Whisk together until smooth and glossy.

4. In another bowl, sift together the pastry flour, salt and baking powder. Set aside.

5. In the bowl of a stand mixer fitted with the whisk attachment, whip the egg whites until frothy. Slowly add the icing sugar and whip until it reaches stiff peaks.

6. Whisk one-quarter of the flour mixture into the egg yolk mixture, followed by one-quarter of the cocoa mixture. Repeat, alternating between the two, until all mixtures are fully combined. Gently fold in the egg white mixture to create a batter.

7. Pour the batter into a 9- by 13-inch baking pan. Do not grease or spray the sides of the pan, as the cake needs to stick to climb up the sides.

8. Bake the cake for 55 to 60 minutes, until it has a nice golden color.

9. While the cake is baking, make the milk mixture. Combine the evaporated milk, condensed milk and chocolate milk in a bowl and whisk well. Warm the mixture in the microwave or in a pot over low heat until lukewarm.

10. As soon as the cake is out of the oven, use a fork to prick holes all over, which will allow the milk mixture to soak in. Then, pour the milk mixture evenly over it, covering its entire surface. Start by pouring in the middle of the cake, then move out to the corners in circular motions. Place the cake in the fridge for at least 1 hour or overnight to absorb all the milk.

11. Just before you're ready to serve, make the topping. Whisk together the cream, icing sugar and cocoa powder to medium peaks. Spread evenly all over the cooled cake and garnish with chocolate shavings.

Dark Chocolate Cheesecake

Makes one 6-inch cheesecake

Prep Time: 15 minutes, plus 2 hours chilling

Cook Time: 50 to 60 minutes

Who doesn't love cheesecake? It's one of my favorites. In our pastry shop, cheesecake is one of the most popular items we offer. If you're not a fan, it may be because you've had one that was dry and crumbly. This recipe delivers a cheesecake that's moist and delicious. It's also full of chocolate goodness, which perfectly balances the tartness of the cream cheese.

Chocolate Base

1 tablespoon + 1 teaspoon (20 g) unsalted butter, melted

1¼ teaspoons granulated sugar

1 cup (120 g) crushed chocolate cookie crumbs

Filling

1⅛ cups (250 g) cream cheese

6 tablespoons (75 g) granulated sugar

7 oz (200 g) dark chocolate, melted (see page 7)

1 large egg

2 large egg yolks

1 teaspoon vanilla extract

⅓ cup (75 ml) heavy cream

Sour Cream Topping

¾ cup (200 g) sour cream

1¼ tablespoons (10 g) Dutch-process cocoa powder

1½ tablespoons (20 g) granulated sugar

NOTE

Always check your cheesecake while it's baking. Depending on your oven, it may take longer to cook, but be careful not to overcook, or it will crack and dry out.

1. Preheat the oven to 325°F. Spray or grease a 6-inch springform pan.

2. For the base, combine the melted butter with the sugar and cookie crumbs in a large bowl.

3. Transfer the base mixture to the springform pan and evenly distribute it over the bottom and up the sides as well. Using the flat bottom of a glass, press the crumbs to compress them and hold the shape.

4. Bake the base in the oven for 10 minutes to set. Remove from the oven and cool on a wire rack, leaving it in the pan.

5. Lower the oven temperature to 210°F.

6. For the filling, place the cream cheese and sugar in the bowl of a stand mixer fitted with the paddle attachment. Beat them together on medium speed until light and fluffy.

7. Add the melted chocolate and beat until fully combined, scraping down the bowl as needed. Add the egg, egg yolks and vanilla and mix well. Scrape the bowl to remove any batter stuck to the bottom, then continue mixing to achieve a creamy texture. Add the cream and blend well.

8. Pour the filling mixture into the pan. Evenly spread it across the base, using a small offset spatula. Place the cheesecake on a baking sheet and bake for about 45 minutes. Always check cheesecake 5 minutes before it should be done, to make sure it's not overcooking. To check for doneness, gently shake the pan. If the filling is set in the middle, it's done.

9. While the cheesecake is baking, make the topping. In a bowl, whisk together by hand the sour cream, cocoa powder and sugar.

10. As soon as the cheesecake is done, remove it from the oven and let cool for 5 minutes. Increase the oven temperature to 325°F.

11. Pour the sour cream mixture evenly over the cheesecake. Return it to the oven for 2 minutes to quickly and lightly set the topping.

12. Remove the cheesecake from the oven and allow it to cool in the pan in the fridge for 2 hours. When it's fully cooled, remove the springform pan and serve.

Chocolate Flapper Pie

Makes one 9-inch pie
Prep Time: 20 minutes, plus 20 minutes chilling
Cook Time: 45 minutes

Pie Crust

⅓ cup (75 g) unsalted butter, melted

¼ cup (50 g) granulated sugar

1½ cups (180 g) crushed chocolate cookie crumbs

Chocolate Custard

½ cup (100 g) granulated sugar

¼ cup (30 g) cornstarch

4 large egg yolks

2¼ cups (560 ml) whole milk

4.5 oz (120 g) milk couverture chocolate, chopped

1.6 oz (40 g) dark couverture chocolate, chopped

¼ cup (60 g) unsalted butter, room temperature

Swiss Meringue

4 large egg whites

1 cup (200 g) granulated sugar

Pinch kosher salt

⅛ teaspoon lemon juice

NOTE

This pie is best eaten at room temperature. If left in the fridge too long, the sugar in the meringue will melt and leak and the crust will become soggy.

I was first introduced to flapper pie while filming a cooking show on the Canadian prairies. The custard pie was to die for—full of flavor, yet so simple to make—and I had to recreate it once I got home. The custard filling is set in a wonderful chocolate crumb crust and finished with a sweet, silky meringue. It's a truly satisfying and delicious combination of textures and flavors!

1. Preheat the oven to 325°F. Spray or grease a 9-inch pie plate (it should be about 1 inch deep).

2. For the crust, combine the melted butter, sugar and cookie crumbs in a bowl. Pour the mixture into the pie pan and distribute it evenly right up to the rim. Using the flat bottom of a glass, gently compress the crumbs against the bottom of the dish and up the sides.

3. Bake the crust for 10 minutes. Remove from the oven and allow to cool.

4. Meanwhile, for the custard base, whisk together the sugar, cornstarch and egg yolks.

5. Place the milk in a medium pot and bring to a boil on high heat. Once it's boiling, slowly pour half of the milk into the egg yolk mixture, whisking continuously to temper the eggs. Then pour the egg mixture into the remaining milk in the pot.

6. Place the pot on medium heat and whisk continuously, until the mixture becomes thick and starts to bubble. Reduce the heat to low and cook for another 2 minutes, whisking constantly. Remove from the heat and immediately whisk in the chopped milk and dark chocolates, until fully melted. Using an immersion blender, add the butter and blend to create a smooth-textured emulsion.

7. Pour the hot custard into the pie crust and flatten it to make it level. Refrigerate until set, about 20 minutes.

8. While the custard sets, make the Swiss meringue. Place the egg whites and sugar in a bowl set over a pot of simmering water to create a double boiler. Whisk constantly until the sugar has completely dissolved and the mixture looks a bit milky, about 6 minutes.

9. Transfer the egg white mixture to the bowl of a stand mixer fitted with the whisk attachment, or use a hand mixer. Add the salt and lemon juice. Whisk the egg whites until they come to full volume with stiff peaks and have cooled down fully.

10. Dollop the meringue evenly over the custard filling. You can also use a kitchen torch to lightly brûlée the meringue, giving it a toasted marshmallow look.

Chocolate Lava Cakes

Makes four 6-ounce servings
Prep Time: 10 minutes
Cook Time: 10 to 12 minutes

---

4 oz (120 g) dark chocolate

½ cup (115 g) unsalted butter, room temperature

¼ cup (50 g) granulated sugar

3 large egg yolks

2 large eggs

4½ tablespoons (40 g) all-purpose flour

1 teaspoon vanilla extract

Pinch kosher salt

Icing sugar, for dusting

I think lava cakes are so popular because they offer the best of all worlds. They were certainly a go-to dessert in most of the restaurants I worked in during my career. They're both a cake and a soufflé, wrapped around a comforting warm liquid center. Cutting into one is like opening a present to reveal the unexpected gift inside. On top of that, while it might seem complex, this is actually an easy and fun dessert to make.

1. Preheat the oven to 450°F. Spray or butter 4 ramekins.

2. Chop the chocolate. Place it in a heatproof, microwave-safe mixing bowl with the butter and melt in the microwave in 30-second increments (see page 7). Whisk to combine fully, then whisk in the sugar, egg yolks and whole eggs. Add the flour, vanilla and salt and whisk just to combine.

3. Divide the mixture evenly among the ramekins, place the ramekins on a baking sheet and bake for 10 to 12 minutes. As soon as the tops and edges form a crust, remove the cakes from the oven. Carefully invert them on a wire rack, being careful not to break the crust.

4. Dust with icing sugar and serve while still warm, with vanilla ice cream to complement the gooey center.

No-Bake Chocolate Ganache Tart

Makes one 9-inch tart

Prep Time: 30 minutes, plus 1 hour, 30 minutes chilling

Cook Time: 20 minutes

Tart Shell

½ cup (115 g) unsalted butter, room temperature

¼ teaspoon kosher salt

½ cup (65 g) icing sugar

1 large egg, room temperature

1⅓ cups + 2 tablespoons (215 g) all-purpose flour

⅛ cup (15 g) almond flour

⅛ cup (15 g) Dutch-process cocoa powder

Ganache Filling

2 gelatin sheets or ½ tablespoon (4 g) gelatin powder

2.3 oz (65 g) dark chocolate

⅔ cup (150 ml) whole milk

1½ teaspoons light corn syrup

⅔ cup + 1 teaspoon (155 ml) heavy cream

NOTE

If there is any leftover ganache, fill a piping bag and, once the tart has fully set, pipe the ganache over the top in a circular motion to give it a special finish.

I enjoy tarts filled with custard and fruit, particularly in the summer, but I've always been a fan of the simple chocolate tart, which is a perfect treat all year round. This tart is rich and silky, with a light crust that crumbles in your mouth.

1. For the tart dough, combine the butter, salt and icing sugar in the bowl of a stand mixer fitted with the paddle attachment. Cream until light and fluffy. Add the egg and combine until fluffy.

2. Sift together the all-purpose flour, almond flour and cocoa powder and add to the butter mixture. Mix until it just comes together. Remove the dough from the bowl, flatten into a square, wrap with plastic wrap and place in the fridge for 20 minutes. (The dough will be easier to roll out when cold.)

3. While the dough is resting, preheat the oven to 325°F, and prepare the filling.

4. Bloom the gelatin sheets in cold water until fully hydrated, about 5 minutes. Remove the sheets and squeeze out any excess water. If using powdered gelatin, the ratio is 5 parts water to 1 part powdered gelatin.

5. Melt the chocolate in a small, microwave-safe bowl (see page 7) and set aside.

6. Combine the milk and corn syrup in a separate microwave-safe bowl. Heat on high power for 40 seconds, so the milk gets hot and melts the corn syrup. Add the bloomed gelatin to the hot milk to dissolve.

7. Strain the milk mixture over the melted chocolate. Emulsify with an immersion blender until smooth and silky. Add the cold cream and blend to fully combine. Set the mixture aside.

8. Remove the dough from the fridge, lightly flour your work surface and roll out the dough to a circle ⅛ inch thick and about 12 inches in diameter—wide enough to fit into the tart pan with some overhang.

9. Spray a 9-inch tart pan with nonstick spray and then line it with the dough, letting it overhang the sides. Trim off any excess.

10. Line the dough with aluminum foil and fill with baking beans. Bake in the preheated oven for 10 minutes. Remove the baking beans and bake for another 3 to 5 minutes, until the middle of the shell looks dull. Remove from the oven and cool completely.

11. Fill the tart with the ganache filling right to the rim, then spread it evenly, using a small offset spatula. Refrigerate until set, about 1½ hours.

Dark Chocolate Gâteau

Makes one 3-layer, 9-inch cake
Prep Time: 1 hour
Cook Time: 15 minutes

½ batch Chocolate Mirror Glaze (page 244)

Chocolate Ganache Topper

3.2 oz (90 g) dark chocolate, chopped

½ cup (125 ml) heavy cream

1½ tablespoons (22 ml) corn syrup

Chocolate Swiss Buttercream

3 oz (85 g) dark chocolate

1½ cups (340 g) unsalted butter, cold

4 large egg whites

1 cup (200 g) granulated sugar

¼ teaspoon kosher salt

Chocolate Sponge

13.2 oz (375 g) dark chocolate

10 large eggs

Pinch kosher salt

¾ cup + 1 tablespoon (160 g) granulated sugar

1¾ cups (400 g) unsalted butter, room temperature

1 cup (150 g) all-purpose flour

If you are looking for that perfect chocolate cake, look no further. This decadent cake is rich in chocolate, with a moist chocolate sponge, silky smooth icing and a rich ganache that melts in the mouth. But be prepared, and give yourself time to make it. Yes, this cake can be challenging to create, but it will make you a better baker and inspire you to create even more showstoppers.

1. For the ganache topper, place the chopped chocolate in a bowl and set aside.

2. Combine the cream and corn syrup in a pot and bring to a boil over medium heat. Once boiling, remove from the heat and pour the mixture over the chopped chocolate. Whisk together to create a smooth consistency. Set aside in the fridge until ready to assemble the cake.

3. For the buttercream, melt the chocolate in the microwave (see page 7), using a digital thermometer to make sure it reaches 104°F. Set aside.

4. Chop the butter into cubes and set aside.

5. Bring a small pot of water to a simmer. Combine the egg whites and sugar in a heatproof bowl. Once the water is simmering, place the bowl over the pot, ensuring that it doesn't make contact with the water. Whisk the egg whites and sugar continuously until the sugar dissolves and the mixture reaches 167°F on a digital thermometer. The mixture should start to look translucent.

6. Transfer the egg white mixture immediately to the bowl of a stand mixer fitted with the whisk attachment. Add the salt. Mix on high speed to cool down the mixture and achieve full volume with stiff peaks.

7. Reduce the speed to medium and slowly add the butter in thirds, mixing until fully combined after each addition. Increase the speed to high and whip the mixture until it reaches full volume.

8. Once the buttercream has reached full volume, reduce the speed to low and slowly pour in the melted chocolate. Stop the mixer and scrape down the sides to incorporate all the ingredients. Increase the speed to high and whip again for 5 minutes to achieve full volume. Set aside in a clean bowl at room temperature.

9. For the sponge, preheat the oven to 325°F and line a 13- by 18-inch baking sheet with parchment paper.

10. Chop and melt the chocolate in a microwave-safe bowl (see page 7). Set aside.

Continued . . .

11. Separate the eggs, placing the yolks and whites in separate bowls.

12. Transfer the egg whites to the clean bowl of your stand mixer and add the salt. Beat with the whisk attachment on medium speed until they increase in volume and look frothy. With the mixer running, slowly and gently add the sugar until incorporated. Increase the speed to high and whisk until the mixture reaches full volume and stiff peaks. Return to their bowl and set aside.

13. Place the butter in the bowl that the egg whites were whipped in. Using the paddle attachment, whip the butter on high speed until light and fluffy. Scrape down the bowl and whip for another 30 seconds.

14. Add the egg yolks, one at a time, mixing until fully incorporated. Scrape down the bowl and whip for another 30 seconds. Add in the flour and mix on low speed until fully incorporated.

15. With the mixer still on low speed, pour in the melted chocolate. Whip until incorporated. Scrape down the bowl and whip again for another 30 seconds to create a smooth texture.

16. Remove the bowl from the mixer, add one-quarter of the egg whites, and beat them into the mixture to lighten its texture. Then fold in the remaining whites to form a light sponge batter. Spread the batter on the lined baking sheet and bake for 15 minutes.

17. Remove from the oven and allow the sponge to cool to room temperature on the sheet. Then place the sheet in the fridge for 10 minutes to cool fully and set (this will make it easier to cut).

18. To assemble the cake, cut out 2 pieces, each measuring 9 inches square. Piece together the remaining cake to form a third 9-inch square.

19. Place the pieced-together cake square at the bottom of a 9-inch square cake ring. Portion out $^2/_3$ cup (85 g) of buttercream and spread it evenly over the cake. Lay the second sponge square on top and repeat the process. Then add the third square and remaining buttercream. The final layer of buttercream must be completely flat. Place the cake ring in the fridge for 10 minutes to set the buttercream.

20. While the cake is setting, remove the ganache topper from the fridge. Heat in the microwave on medium power in 30-second increments, until the ganache is pourable but not hot. Its ideal temperature is 95°F.

21. Remove the cake from the fridge. Pour the ganache over it to form a flat, even layer. Place the cake in the freezer for 1 hour to set.

22. Once the cake is set, remove the cake ring, using a knife to score around the inside of the frame. Place the cake back in the fridge.

23. Warm the chocolate glaze in the microwave on medium power in 30-second increments until it reaches 95°F.

24. Take the cake out of the fridge. Using a pastry brush, brush a thin coat of glaze over the top of the cake to give it a shine. Cut and serve at room temperature.

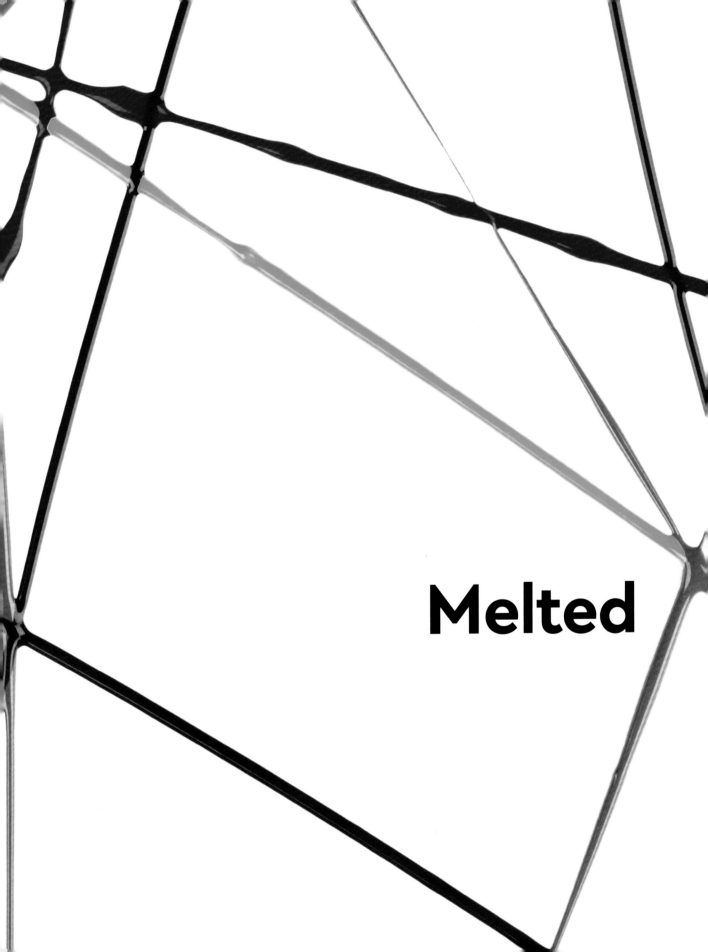

Melted

Dark Chocolate Salted Caramel Brigadeiros

Makes 20 chocolates
Prep Time: 15 minutes
Cook Time: 20 minutes

---

14 oz (414 ml) can condensed milk

1 tablespoon (15 g) unsalted butter, room temperature

⅛ teaspoon kosher salt

2 teaspoons Dutch-process cocoa powder, sifted

7 oz (200 g) dark chocolate, melted (see page 7)

Coating

Cocoa powder, ground chocolate, sprinkles or crushed nuts

Brigadeiros look like truffles, but they are a specific type of chocolate treat from Brazil. They are made with condensed milk and butter, and the outside is soft just like the inside, whereas a truffle is covered in a thin shell of chocolate. These chocolates are a great project to make with the kiddos. Have fun and change up the coating with sprinkles, chocolate shavings or crushed nuts.

1. In a pot set over low heat, combine the condensed milk, butter and salt. Heat until fully melted.

2. Stir in the sifted cocoa powder. Add the melted chocolate and cook until the mixture starts to thicken and become shiny, about 5 minutes. The temperature should reach 180°F.

3. Remove the pot from the heat and pour the mixture onto a baking sheet lined with parchment paper. Allow it to cool and set completely at room temperature.

4. Once the mixture is cool, portion it out into 1 tablespoon scoops. Roll the portions into balls.

5. Place the desired coating in a small bowl or on a shallow plate and roll the balls in it to coat them completely.

6. Store the brigadeiros in an airtight container at room temperature.

Dark Chocolate Truffles

Makes 30 truffles
Prep Time: 2 hours
Cook Time: 8 minutes

8.1 oz (230 g) dark chocolate

½ cup + ⅓ cup (205 ml) heavy cream

1 tablespoon (20 g) corn syrup

1 tablespoon (15 g) unsalted butter, room temperature

7 oz (200 g) dark chocolate, tempered (see page 8)

¼ cup (30 g) Dutch-process cocoa powder, for rolling

There is nothing more elegant to serve than a simple chocolate truffle. A truffle is traditionally made with a ganache (a mixture of cream and chocolate), then formed into a ball and coated in tempered chocolate to give it a shell. Creamy chocolate truffles explode with flavor and melt in your mouth. They were my first introduction to the world of chocolate making. I had to master the art of pure chocolate ganache in order to learn the techniques for building a wide variety of ganaches, so this recipe will always have a special place in my heart.

1. Start by placing the chocolate in a microwave-safe bowl. Melt it in the microwave in 10-second increments, so you do not burn the chocolate.

2. Combine the cream and corn syrup in a small pot and bring to a boil.

3. Stir the cream mixture into the melted chocolate, one-third at a time. Once incorporated, use an immersion blender to emulsify the mixture fully. You want a glossy finish.

4. Set the ganache aside with a digital thermometer in it. Allow it to cool to 104°F.

5. Once the ganache has reached the desired temperature (or below), add the butter and use an immersion blender to emulsify the mixture.

6. Cover the bowl with plastic wrap and allow the ganache to set slightly for about 2 hours. If you are not going to use it right away, you can store it in the fridge, and place it on the counter to warm up for 30 minutes before piping.

7. Transfer the ganache into a piping bag and line a baking sheet with parchment paper. Pipe mini ganache "kisses" onto the lined baking sheet. Allow the ganache to set fully, then roll each chocolate kiss into a ball.

8. Place the tempered chocolate in a large bowl. Place the cocoa powder in a separate shallow bowl.

9. Place a small amount of tempered chocolate in the palm of your hand and roll each truffle in it to coat in a thin layer of chocolate. Immediately place the truffle into the bowl with the cocoa powder and swirl the bowl in circular motions to coat completely. Remove the truffle and repeat the process until all the kisses are coated. Use more cocoa powder if needed, then serve at room temperature.

NOTE

You can refrigerate these truffles, but they are best eaten at room temperature. If storing in the fridge, allow them to come to room temperature before enjoying— ideally between 65° and 68°F for the best texture.

Peppermint Patties

Makes 30 patties

Prep Time: 25 minutes

---

5 ¾ cups (750 g) icing sugar

1½ cups (350 ml) condensed milk

1 tablespoon (15 ml) peppermint extract

¼ teaspoon kosher salt

15 oz (450 g) dark chocolate, tempered (see page 8)

I don't think I've ever met a person who doesn't like peppermint patties. They're a favorite with my family during the holidays, but I love them so much that I make sure they're available year-round at our pastry shop. I use a high-percentage dark chocolate (70% or more) to balance the sweetness of the filling. They have a long shelf life if stored in an airtight container, so you can make them before the hectic pace of the holiday season begins. These are delicious served with vanilla ice cream.

1. Combine the icing sugar, condensed milk, peppermint extract and salt in the bowl of a stand mixer fitted with the paddle attachment. Mix until well combined and the mixture looks like a dough, about 5 minutes.

2. Remove the mixture from the bowl. If you're making it ahead, wrap it in plastic wrap. When ready, heavily dust your work surface with icing sugar. Place the mixture on the work surface and heavily dust the top with icing sugar. Roll out the mixture to about ⅛ inch thick, making sure to constantly around move the mixture and dust with additional icing sugar as needed, so it doesn't stick to the work surface or the rolling pin.

3. Use a 2-inch circle cutter to cut out pieces. Place them on a baking sheet lined with parchment paper to dry out—this is to help prevent any bending when you pick them up later to dip in the chocolate. Gather up the remaining mixture and roll it out again, using additional icing sugar as needed, and repeat the process.

4. Place the tempered chocolate in a large, shallow bowl so it's deep enough for you to submerge the patties. First use a pastry brush to apply a thin layer of chocolate to both sides of each patty. This will give it structure and durability for when you dip it into the bowl of chocolate. Once the thin layer has dried, individually submerge each patty in the tempered chocolate, then place on a clean piece of parchment paper to dry completely. Store in an airtight container.

NOTE

Peppermint patties are great for the holidays, so get creative with different shapes of cookie cutters.

Double Chocolate Marshmallows

Makes sixteen 2-inch squares
Prep Time: 5 minutes
Cook Time: 20 minutes

---

12 gelatin sheets or 2 tablespoons (16 g) gelatin powder

1½ cups (300 g) granulated sugar

½ cup (150 g) honey

4½ tablespoons (90 g) light corn syrup

⅓ cup (75 ml) water

½ cup (60 g) Dutch-process cocoa powder, sifted

Optional Coatings

¼ cup (30 g) icing sugar

¼ cup (30 g) cornstarch

4 teaspoons (8 g) Dutch-process cocoa powder

OR

18 oz (500 g) dark chocolate, tempered (see page 8)

NOTE

You want the marshmallow to be warm when transferring it from the bowl to the pan, so that it's easier to remove from the mixer. Once the mixture cools it becomes sticky and difficult to flatten.

You can store these marshmallows for a several weeks in an airtight container at room temperature, because they don't contain egg whites.

These treats are versatile. You can eat them, bake with them, roast them or melt them in hot chocolate for an extra hit of chocolate flavor. I love this recipe because it's great to make with kids, especially during the holidays. You can cut out different shapes with cookie cutters, dip them in chocolate to give them crunch or just leave them plain, like the ones you buy in the store.

1. Bloom the gelatin sheets in cold water until fully hydrated, about 5 minutes. Remove the sheets and squeeze out any excess water. If using powdered gelatin, the ratio is 5 parts water to 1 part powdered gelatin.

2. Line an 8-inch square baking pan with parchment paper, across the bottom and up the sides. Grease the parchment with canola oil or nonstick spray. If the paper is not greased, you won't be able to peel off the marshmallows.

3. Combine the sugar, honey, corn syrup and water in a medium pot set over medium-high heat. Using a candy thermometer, cook until the mixture reaches the soft-ball stage, 245°F.

4. Remove the mixture from the heat and transfer to the bowl of a stand mixer fitted with the whisk attachment. Add the bloomed gelatin and sifted cocoa powder. Mix on low speed until the gelatin is fully melted. Turn off the mixer and scrape down the bowl to fully incorporate if necessary. Turn the mixer speed to high and whisk until the mixture starts to thicken and lighten in color, about 6 minutes. It should stream off the whisk, creating ribbons on the surface. Do not overmix or let cool completely, as the marshmallow will become too thick and difficult to remove from the bowl.

5. Transfer the marshmallow to the baking pan. Cut an 8-inch square piece of greased or sprayed parchment paper and press it down over the marshmallow to level and flatten the surface.

6. Allow the marshmallow to set completely. Remove from the pan, grease a knife and cut the marshmallow into sixteen 2-inch squares.

7. If you'd like to dust the marshmallows, combine the icing sugar, cornstarch and cocoa powder in a bowl. Drop in the marshmallows, turning them to cover completely, then set aside on a wire rack. You can also coat the marshmallows in tempered chocolate; set them aside on a piece of parchment paper to cool, then store in an airtight container at room temperature.

Chocolate Sea Foam

Makes one 9- by 13-inch slab

Prep Time: 5 minutes

Cook Time: 12 minutes

1½ cups + 2 tablespoons (325 g) granulated sugar

½ cup (150 g) honey

6 tablespoons (120 g) corn syrup

⅓ cup (75 ml) water

1 tablespoon + 1 teaspoon (20 g) baking soda

18 oz (500 g) dark chocolate, tempered (see page 8)

This is the most delicious science experiment you'll ever eat. The chemical reaction that occurs when you mix the ingredients gives this treat its texture and crunch. The secret to its subtle sweet flavor, though, is the honey. And, of course, everything is better coated with a little chocolate, which also helps preserve the texture. Don't be afraid to make this—you'll love the result. Try a little crushed over ice cream.

1. Line a 9- by 13-inch baking pan with parchment paper, across the bottom and up the sides.

2. Combine the sugar, honey, corn syrup and water in a medium pot set over medium heat. Cook until the mixture reaches a golden caramel color and the temperature reaches 300°F on a candy thermometer, 3 to 5 minutes.

3. Once a caramel color has been achieved, remove the pot from the heat and immediately whisk in the baking soda, making sure there are no lumps. The caramel will bubble up because of the chemical reaction. Pour the mixture into the lined baking pan and let cool at room temperature.

4. Once it's completely cooled, break apart the sea foam in big chunks and set aside. The pieces don't have to be uniform.

5. Place the tempered chocolate in a large, shallow bowl and coat each piece of sea foam. Store in a cool, dry place in an airtight container.

NOTE

If left uncovered, sea foam will pick up moisture from the air and become soft and very chewy.

Fruit and Nut Chocolate Bark

Makes one 13- by 18-inch slab

Prep Time: 25 minutes

½ cup (55 g) peanuts, or whatever nuts you like

⅔ cup (50 g) candied lemon peel

⅔ cup (50 g) candied orange peel

⅓ cup (50 g) raisins

⅓ cup (50 g) dried cranberries

32.5 oz (900 g) dark chocolate, tempered (see page 8)

This chocolate bark is perfect to have around the house as a healthful snack. Pack a couple of pieces in the kids' lunchbox for school or in your bag for a snack on the go. The great thing about this recipe is that you can add just about anything to the bark. Get inspired by the different seasons and holidays!

1. Preheat the oven to 325°F. Place the peanuts on a baking sheet and toast for 10 minutes. Then roughly chop the nuts and allow to cool.

2. Cut up the lemon and orange peel to the size you desire. Place in a bowl with the raisins, dried cranberries and chopped peanuts and mix well.

3. Line a 13- by 18-inch baking sheet with parchment paper.

4. Place the tempered chocolate in a large bowl. Add one-third of the fruit-and-nut mixture and mix well. Transfer to the lined baking sheet and spread it to about ⅛ inch thick. Quickly distribute the remaining fruit-and-nut mixture evenly over the chocolate so the fruits and nuts stick to it (see Note).

5. Allow the bark to set, then break into pieces. Store in an airtight container.

NOTE

You need to move fast when distributing the fruit and nuts over the chocolate. If you don't, the chocolate will set before they can stick.

Chocolate English Toffee

Makes one 13- by 18-inch slab

Prep Time: 5 minutes

Cook Time: 40 minutes

1½ cups (300 g) granulated sugar

1 cup (225 g) unsalted butter, room temperature

2 tablespoons + 1 teaspoon (50 g) honey

¾ teaspoon kosher salt

18 oz (500 g) dark chocolate, tempered (see page 8)

When I was growing up, someone always brought a version of English toffee to our family gatherings, especially during the holidays, and it was one of my favorite sweets to reach for in the candy bowl. These days I make three different versions in my pastry shop, and they fly off the shelves. This toffee crumbles in your mouth and leaves nutty caramel notes on your tongue. I find that pairing it with dark chocolate adds a slight bitterness to offset the sweetness in every bite.

1. Line a 13- by 18-inch baking sheet with parchment paper. Make sure the sheet isn't warped, as you want the toffee to dry completely flat. You can also place a large piece of parchment paper directly on your counter in order to ensure that the toffee dries flat.

2. Combine the sugar, butter, honey and salt in a medium pot set over medium heat. Cook, whisking continuously, for 8 to 10 minutes or until the mixture reaches 300°F on a candy thermometer. Don't step away from the pot, as it can burn easily.

3. Once the toffee mixture reaches temperature, pour it directly onto the parchment paper. Spread it very thin, to about $1/16$ inch thick. Let the toffee cool completely for 25 to 30 minutes.

4. Place the tempered chocolate in a glass measuring cup with a spout. Pour half of the chocolate over the toffee and use a small offset spatula to spread it evenly in a thin layer. Allow to set. Then flip the toffee and repeat on the other side. Once the chocolate is fully set, break the toffee into pieces and store in an airtight container.

NOTE

You can add nuts to this toffee. Crush any type of nut and sprinkle it in a thin layer over the chocolate before it fully hardens and sets.

Salted Chocolate Chewy Caramels

Makes one 9- by 13-inch slab
Prep Time: 5 minutes
Cook Time: 1 hour

---

2 cups (500 ml) heavy cream

3½ cups (705 g) granulated sugar

1½ cups (335 g) unsalted butter, room temperature

¾ cup (250 g) corn syrup

18 oz (500 g) dark chocolate, tempered (see page 8)

Flaky salt

NOTE

Do not heat the caramel over 253°F, or it will be too hard to cut and eat. If you do not want to coat the caramels in chocolate, wrap each piece separately in parchment paper or cellophane.

Caramels are one of the most common requests I get as a chocolatier, so they're permanently on my menu. Properly cooked caramels should be elastic and melt in the mouth. If you've eaten mass-produced caramels, you probably remember how much they stick in your teeth. But caramels cooked to the proper temperature should not stick, and these ones are the perfect remedy for any bad experiences you've had in the past! I love to coat caramels in tempered dark chocolate, because the tartness of the chocolate balances the sweetness of the chewy caramel.

1. Line a 9- by 13-inch baking sheet with parchment paper.

2. Place the cream in a medium pot and bring to a boil. Set aside.

3. In a separate pot over medium heat, make a dry caramel with the sugar. Sprinkle one-quarter of the sugar into the pot. Slowly move the pot in a circular motion to evenly distribute the sugar and allow it to melt fully. Once it's melted, add another one-quarter of the sugar without stirring, and repeat the process, until all the sugar has been added. Once all the sugar is melted, slowly stir it to evenly distribute the caramel color. Cook until a medium golden color.

4. Slowly pour one-quarter of the cream into the caramel and stir well. The mixture will rise and then deflate. Add another one-quarter of the cream, then repeat, until all the cream has been incorporated.

5. Heat the caramel-cream mixture to 230°F on a candy thermometer. Add the butter and corn syrup.

6. Stirring continuously, heat the mixture to 250°F, making sure it doesn't burn on the bottom.

7. Once temperature has been reached, pour the caramel onto the lined baking sheet. Allow it to set for 1 hour at room temperature. Once cool, remove the caramel from the pan and cut the slab into 1-inch or 2-inch squares. Using a metal spatula, transfer them to a piece of parchment paper without touching them with your fingers.

8. Place the tempered chocolate in a large bowl. Using a fork, dip each caramel into the chocolate. Let as much excess chocolate as possible drip off, then place the caramel back on the parchment paper. Sprinkle with a few flakes of sea salt and let set completely before serving or storing for later.

Chocolate Saltwater Taffy

Makes 50 to 60 pieces
Prep Time: 1 hour
Cook Time: 15 minutes

---

2 tablespoons (15 g) cornstarch

1¾ cups (350 g) granulated sugar

²/₃ cup (150 ml) condensed milk

²/₃ cup (150 ml) water

1 cup (325 g) corn syrup

2 tablespoons (30 g) unsalted
butter, room temperature

1 teaspoon kosher salt

9 oz (250 g) dark chocolate,
chopped

This is a fun recipe to make, because you get to use your hands and feel like a real candy maker. You get to pull and stretch the taffy, and the more you do it, the better it'll be. As you can guess, kids love to help with this one. It feels like playing with Play-Doh, but it tastes so much better!

1. Line a large baking sheet with parchment paper or a Silpat mat.

2. Sift the cornstarch into a medium bowl. Add the sugar and whisk together to combine and remove any lumps. Transfer to a medium pot set over medium-low heat. Add the condensed milk and water, whisking to combine fully. Then add the corn syrup, butter and salt.

3. Cook the mixture until it reaches 250°F on a candy thermometer, whisking continuously so the mixture doesn't burn on the bottom.

4. Once temperature has been reached, mix in the chopped chocolate until it has melted fully. Then, pour the taffy onto the lined sheet. Let it cool until you can handle it, about 10 minutes.

5. Form the taffy into a ball, then start stretching it to incorporate air. As it stretches it will become elastic, with little air bubbles lightening it in color and softness. Pull and stretch the taffy for about 20 minutes.

6. Once you have achieved the desired consistency, take portions of the taffy and roll into 1-inch-diameter logs. Cut the logs into pieces about 1½ inches long, form them into rectangles, and immediately wrap in waxed paper.

NOTE

The taffy must be wrapped right away or stored in an airtight container. If left exposed to the air at room temperature, it will harden.

Chocolate Fudge

Makes 20 to 25 pieces
Prep Time: 8 minutes
Cook Time: 25 to 30 minutes

---

4 cups (800 g) granulated sugar

½ cup (156 g) corn syrup

½ cup (60 g) Dutch-process cocoa powder

Pinch kosher salt

1½ cups (350 ml) whole milk

6.7 oz (190 g) dark chocolate, chopped

¼ cup (60 g) unsalted butter, room temperature

1 teaspoon vanilla extract

Fudge is one of those confections I've always loved making, because I'm drawn to the science behind it and the technique required to make it—the sugar crystallization, the stirring process, the right temperature, and more. Fudge can be unforgiving, but if executed correctly, the texture is unbelievable. It's creamy and melts in your mouth, has a great shelf life and offers the opportunity to introduce extreme flavor profiles. Over the years I've tried recipes that produced dry, grainy, crumbly fudge, but this one is just right—the results are soft, creamy and unforgettable.

1. In a large pot set over medium heat, combine the sugar, corn syrup, cocoa powder, salt and milk. Cook, whisking occasionally, until the mixture reaches 239°F on a candy thermometer, which should take 10 to 12 minutes.

2. Place the chopped chocolate in the bowl of a stand mixer fitted with the paddle attachment. Once the milk mixture reaches temperature, pour it over the chocolate and whip for 3 minutes, until the milk has slightly cooled and the chocolate has melted. Add the butter and vanilla.

3. Continue to whip the fudge mixture on medium speed for about 8 minutes, until it loses its sheen and starts to thicken.

4. While the fudge is mixing, line a 9-inch square baking pan with parchment paper.

5. Once the fudge is properly mixed, pour it into the baking pan and spread it out evenly with an offset spatula. Allow it to crystallize and set for up to 1 hour, then cut into small squares.

NOTE

Temperature is key in making fudge. If the mixture is heated beyond 239°F, it will because grainy and break apart.

Chocolate-Coated Candied Peel

Makes 8 ounces

Prep Time: 10 minutes, plus 30 minutes drying

Cook Time: 40 minutes

---

2 large oranges, lemons or grapefruits

2 cups (500 ml) water

1 cup (200 g) granulated sugar

7 oz (200 g) dark chocolate, tempered (see page 8)

Fruit pairs especially well with chocolate because it accentuates any fruity notes in the chocolate. See the chocolate-tasting notes on page 23 for some ideas about the flavors you can find in your chocolate. Here I'm using fresh citrus peel, but whether you use candied, dried or fresh fruit, it all tastes great with a little chocolate.

1. Slice a small amount off the top and the bottom of the oranges to make flat surfaces. Then carefully cut down the length of each orange to remove the peel and pith, making sure not to cut into the flesh.

2. Slice the orange peels into strips ¼ inch wide.

3. Place the peels in a pot and add water to cover. Bring the water to a boil.

4. Strain and discard the water. Repeat the process, straining off the water a second time. This removes the bitterness of the orange peel. Eat the orange itself as a snack while you wait!

5. Add the sugar and 2 cups fresh water to the peels in the pot. Bring the mixture to boil and then reduce the heat to a simmer. Continue simmering the mixture for 30 minutes. The peels should become translucent and the simple syrup will have evaporated slightly.

6. Remove the pot from the heat and let sit for 10 minutes.

7. Remove the peels from the syrup and dry on a wire rack for 30 minutes or up to 24 hours, until the peels have crystallized and dried.

8. Place the tempered chocolate in a cup or bowl. Dip the peels halfway into the chocolate and place on a baking sheet lined with parchment paper to cool.

NOTE

Candied fruit peel can be preserved in the simple syrup you cooked it in for up to 3 months in the fridge. Whenever you feel like chocolate-coated fruit peel, take some out of the fridge, dry them on a wire rack and dip them in melted chocolate.

Chocolate Coconut Bars

Makes 30 bars

Prep Time: 5 minutes + 2 hours for resting

Cook Time: 5 minutes

---

24 oz (680 g) white chocolate

1 cup (250 ml) coconut milk

¼ cup (60 ml) heavy cream

2½ tablespoons (50 g) corn syrup

½ cup (115 g) unsalted butter, room temperature

6 cups (600 g) shredded coconut

3.5 oz (100 g) dark chocolate

18 oz (500 g) dark chocolate, tempered (see page 8)

If you like coconut, you're going to love these bars. Coconut is delicious with chocolate because of the milky, buttery notes they share. And not only is this a great chocolate bar, the coconut filling can also be used in layer cakes or parfaits.

1. Chop the white chocolate into fine pieces and place in a microwave-safe bowl. Melt in the microwave on medium power in 15-second increments. Set aside.

2. Combine the coconut milk, cream and corn syrup in a medium pot. Bring to a boil over medium heat.

3. Pour the hot coconut milk mixture over the chocolate. Using an immersion blender, emulsify to create a smooth texture. Allow the mixture to cool to 104°F and line a 9- by 13-inch baking dish with parchment paper.

4. Once the mixture is cooled, add the butter. Emulsify with the immersion blender, making sure all the butter is incorporated.

5. Fold in the shredded coconut. Transfer the mixture to the lined baking dish and use a small offset spatula to spread out the mixture evenly.

6. Place the dish in the fridge for 2 hours to set.

7. Remove the baking dish from the fridge. Unmold the coconut ganache by quickly flipping the dish upside down onto a fresh sheet of parchment paper.

8. Melt the un-tempered dark chocolate in the microwave (see page 7). Spread about half of it over one side of the ganache to coat. Once the chocolate has set, flip over the ganache and repeat on the other side.

9. Once the chocolate has set, use a heated chef's knife to cut the ganache lengthwise into strips 1 inch wide; you should have 9 pieces. Then cut each strip into pieces about 3 inches long.

10. Place the tempered chocolate in a shallow bowl for dipping.

11. Gently insert a fork into a coconut bar and submerge it in the chocolate. Pull it out slowly, with a twirling motion, to remove any excess chocolate. Place the dipped bar on a baking sheet lined with parchment paper and allow it to set. Repeat the process with the remaining bars.

NOTE

Store the bars in an airtight container in the fridge for up to 3 weeks, or at room temperature for up to 1 week.

Chocolate Caramel Pecan Clusters

Makes about 20 clusters
Prep Time: 5 minutes
Cook Time: 20 minutes

3 cups (300 g) pecan halves

Caramel

¾ cup (175 ml) heavy cream

¼ cup (60 g) unsalted butter, room temperature

1 cup (200 g) granulated sugar

¼ cup (60 ml) water

¼ cup (75 g) honey

18 oz (500 g) milk chocolate, tempered (see page 8)

These chocolate treats are the perfect gift for the holidays, birthday parties and other special events. They are chewy and crunchy, sweet, nutty and salty—the perfect one-bite morsel for a quick chocolate fix.

1. Preheat the oven to 325°F. Line a baking sheet with parchment paper.

2. Toast the pecans on the baking sheet for 8 minutes, until slightly golden and fragrant. Set aside to cool completely.

3. Line a second baking sheet with parchment paper and set aside.

4. Place the cream and butter in a medium pot over medium-high heat. Bring to a boil, stirring until the butter is melted and combined with the cream, then set aside.

5. In a separate pot with a tight-fitting lid, combine the sugar, water and honey. Cover the pot and place over low heat. Let cook for 1 minute, then remove the lid and place a candy thermometer in the pot. (Starting with the lid on helps prevent crystallization.) Cook the mixture just until it reaches 320°F and turns a golden amber color. Keep a close eye on it, as you don't want to overcook it!

6. Immediately, remove the pot from the stove and slowly pour the cream mixture into the sugar syrup, whisking continuously. Do not pour in the cream too quickly, or the sugar will erupt in a boil. Once the cream is fully incorporated, keep whisking.

7. Place the caramel back on the stove over low heat. Cook the caramel until it reaches 245°F on the candy thermometer, which will happen quickly. (This second cook gets you that chewy caramel texture.)

8. As soon as the caramel hits 245°F, remove the pot from the heat and add the pecan halves. Fold in the nuts to distribute them evenly.

9. Using a spoon or a #30 black (1¼ oz) ice-cream scoop, scoop the pecan clusters onto the lined baking sheet, leaving a bit of space between them, and allow to set completely.

10. Place the tempered chocolate in a large, shallow bowl. Gently insert a fork into a cluster and submerge it fully in the chocolate. As you pull it out, twirl the cluster over the bowl to remove any excess chocolate. Transfer the cluster to a clean baking sheet lined with parchment paper to set. Repeat the process with the remaining clusters.

11. Once set, store the clusters in an airtight container for up to 3 weeks, or in the fridge or freezer for up to 1 month.

Cookies, Squares & Bites

Chocolate Raspberry Brownies

Makes 24 brownies
Prep Time: 10 minutes
Cooking Time: 40 to 45 minutes

Brownies

¾ cup (120 g) all-purpose flour

⅓ cup (40 g) Dutch-process cocoa powder

½ teaspoon baking powder

½ teaspoon kosher salt

¾ cup (175 g) butter, room temperature

2 cups (400 g) granulated sugar

2 large eggs, room temperature

2 large egg yolks

6.7 oz (190 g) dark chocolate, chopped

6 oz (170 g) frozen raspberries, roughly chopped

Icing

1 cup (125 g) icing sugar

2 tablespoons (30 g) unsalted butter, room temperature

1 tablespoon (8 g) Dutch-process cocoa powder

3 tablespoons (45 ml) whole milk, hot

1 teaspoon vanilla extract

My mom baked brownies often when I was growing up. She would usually make them just before dinner and set them out to cool as we sat down to eat. The smell of those fresh-baked brownies wafting from the kitchen ensured that everyone ate everything off their plates in order to secure a coveted brownie for dessert. I like to add raspberries to mine, to make them a little different.

1. Preheat the oven to 350°F. Line a 9- by 13-inch baking pan with parchment paper.

2. For the brownies, sift together the flour, cocoa powder and baking powder into a bowl, then add the salt. Set aside.

3. In the bowl of a stand mixer fitted with the paddle attachment, cream together the butter and sugar until fluffy. Add the eggs and egg yolks. Cream on high speed until fully combined, light and fluffy.

4. Reduce the mixer speed to low and slowly add the dry ingredients. Mix until fully incorporated. Fold in the chocolate and frozen raspberries using a spatula.

5. Pour the batter into the lined pan and bake for 40 to 45 minutes, until a skewer inserted in the center comes out clean.

6. While the brownie batter is baking, make the icing. In the stand mixer fitted with the paddle attachment, combine the icing sugar, butter, cocoa powder, hot milk and vanilla. Beat until the mixture becomes soft and creamy.

7. As soon as the brownie mixture is cooked, spread the icing all over the top, while it is still warm. Let cool completely, then cut into 24 squares.

NOTE

Spreading the icing while the cake is still hot will melt it into the brownies and give a nice shine.

Chocolate Lemon Madeleines

Makes about 35 cookies

Prep Time: 10 minutes, plus up to 1 day for resting

Cook Time: 8 to 10 minutes

---

1 cup + 1 teaspoon (155 g) all-purpose flour

1 tablespoon (8 g) Dutch-process cocoa powder

1½ teaspoons baking powder

¼ teaspoon kosher salt

¾ cup (150 g) granulated sugar

4 large eggs, room temperature

⅔ cup + 1 teaspoon (155 g) unsalted butter

1 tablespoon (20 g) honey

1 large lemon, zested

The madeleine is a classic French pastry, but I like to incorporate lemon zest and chocolate. These mini sponge cakes are perfect to serve with tea or coffee. If you want to take your skills to the next level, you can even coat them in tempered chocolate for added texture. The key to a perfect madeleine is to refrigerate the batter for at least 1 hour before baking. Madeleines are best served fresh and warm.

1. Sift together the flour, cocoa powder and baking powder into a bowl. Add the salt.

2. In a separate bowl, whisk together the sugar and eggs until combined.

3. Place the butter, honey and lemon zest in a small pot over low heat to melt the butter (you can also do this in a microwave), then stir to combine.

4. Add the dry ingredients to the egg mixture, one-third at a time, whisking between each addition to form a cakelike batter.

5. Whisk the butter mixture into the batter, one-third at a time, mixing between each addition to combine fully.

6. Transfer the batter to an airtight container with a lid. Let it rest in the fridge for at least 1 hour or up to 24 hours.

7. When ready to bake, preheat the oven to 425°F.

8. Transfer the batter to a piping bag. Prepare a madeleine pan by brushing the cavities with melted butter, then lightly coating the pan with flour. Bang the pan over the sink to remove excess flour.

9. Pipe the batter into the molds to about three-quarters full. Place the batter-filled pan in the fridge for 5 minutes.

10. Once the batter has rested a second time, reduce the oven temperature to 375°F and immediately place the pan in the center of the oven. Bake for 8 to 10 minutes, until the cookies have formed a hump and are a light golden color.

11. Remove the pan from the oven and immediately transfer the madeleines from the molds to a platter. Serve right away.

NOTE

The madeleines have to be removed from the molds right out of the oven, or they will stick.

The batter can be stored for up to 1 week in the fridge. Ideally it should sit for 24 hours, but if you're in a rush and can't wait, allow the batter to sit in the fridge for at least 1 hour.

Chocolate Cookie Caramel Bars

Makes 30 bars
Prep Time: 25 minutes
Cook Time: 45 minutes

Shortbread

1 cup (225 g) unsalted butter, cold

½ cup (65 g) icing sugar

1⅓ cups (200 g) bread flour

½ cup + 2 tablespoons (75 g) ground almonds

1 tablespoon (15 ml) vanilla extract

Caramel

1½ cups (375 ml) heavy cream

5½ tablespoons (100 g) honey

3 tablespoons (45 g) unsalted butter, room temperature

1¾ cups (350 g) granulated sugar

18 oz (500 g) dark couverture chocolate, tempered (see page 8)

My favorite candy bar when I was growing up was a caramel cookie bar. Put your chocolate-making skills to the test with these bars. A tempered chocolate shell encases everything for that telltale crunch.

1. Preheat the oven to 325°F. Grease a 9-inch square baking pan and line the bottom with parchment paper.

2. For the shortbread, combine the butter and icing sugar in the bowl of a stand mixer fitted with the paddle attachment. Cream on high speed, occasionally scraping down the bowl, until light and fluffy.

3. Reduce the speed to low and add the bread flour, ground almonds and vanilla. Mix gently to combine.

4. Remove the dough and press it into the lined baking pan, using your fingers to make it as flat and even as possible.

5. Bake in the oven for 13 to 15 minutes, until the shortbread is a light golden brown. Remove from the oven and let cool completely in the pan.

6. While the shortbread bakes, start the caramel. Place the cream, honey and butter in a medium pot over medium heat. Bring to a boil, stirring to combine as the butter melts, then set aside.

7. In a separate pot, make a dry caramel. Place the pot over medium heat and let it get hot. Start by sprinkling one-quarter of the sugar into the pot. Using a heatproof silicone spatula or wooden spoon, lightly stir the sugar so it melts evenly. When it's close to completely melted, add another one-quarter of the sugar. Repeat the process until all the sugar has been melted. Reduce the heat to low and slowly stir, until no granules remain and the color turns an amber golden brown.

8. Moving quickly so the caramel doesn't burn, temper it with the hot cream. Slowly whisking the caramel, slowly stream in one-quarter of the cream mixture. Whisk until fully incorporated, then add half of the remaining cream. Whisk again and then add the last bit.

9. Increase the heat to medium, still whisking continuously, and cook the caramel to 245°F on a candy thermometer. Once it reaches temperature, pour the caramel over the shortbread. Allow it to set at room temperature for 2 hours.

10. Remove the caramel shortbread from the pan. Cut it into 30 pieces about 1¾ inches wide and 1½ inches long.

11. Place the tempered chocolate in a large bowl. Using forks, dip each bar into the chocolate. Fully submerge, shake off the excess chocolate and place on a baking sheet lined with parchment paper. Once the chocolate has set, store the bars in an airtight container in a cool, dry place. They will last at room temperature for up to 5 days or in the fridge for up to 1 month.

Chocolate Hazelnut Financiers

Makes 12 financiers or 24 mini muffins
Prep Time: 15 minutes
Cook Time: 15 minutes

1½ cups (125 g) ground hazelnuts

1⅓ cups (175 g) icing sugar

⅓ cup (50 g) all-purpose flour

2 tablespoons (15 g) Dutch-process cocoa powder

4 large egg whites

⅔ cup (150 g) unsalted butter

1.6 oz (40 g) dark couverture chocolate, chopped

These mini teacakes, which originated in Paris, are perfect for a tea party. They are traditionally made with almond meal, but I like to use hazelnut meal to give this delicate pastry an earthy undertone that complements the browned butter. When I worked in London at The Wolseley restaurant, these were a staple of their famous high tea.

1. Preheat the oven to 400°F. Spray or grease a financier pan or 2 mini-muffin tins.

2. Combine the ground hazelnuts, icing sugar, flour and cocoa powder in the bowl of a stand mixer fitted with the whisk attachment, or in a bowl to mix by hand.

3. Add the egg whites to the dry ingredients and whisk until fully combined. Scrape down the bowl as needed.

4. Place the butter in a pot set over low heat and allow it to melt. Continue cooking until the butter is slightly browned with a nutty aroma. Add the chopped chocolate and whisk by hand to melt it in.

5. Pour the butter-chocolate mixture into the batter. Mix together very well on low speed. Portion the batter into the pan.

6. Just before you're ready to place the pan in the oven, reduce the temperature to 350°F. Bake the financiers for 12 to 15 minutes, or until light golden brown and a cake tester inserted in the center comes out clean. Remove from the oven and transfer to a wire rack to cool. Store at room temperature for up to 4 days, in the fridge for up to 1 week, or frozen for a few months.

NOTE

If you do not have ground hazelnuts, you can use ground almonds.

Make sure not to overbake the financiers, or they will dry out.

Chocolate Orange Cookies

Makes 20 cookies

Prep Time: 12 minutes, plus 45 minutes for chilling

Cook Time: 8 to 10 minutes

1½ cups (300 g) brown sugar

¾ cup (175 g) unsalted butter, room temperature

1 teaspoon vanilla extract

1 large orange, zested

3 large eggs

1 cup (150 g) all-purpose flour

¼ cup (30 g) natural cocoa powder

1½ teaspoons baking soda

¼ teaspoon kosher salt

5.6 oz (160 g) dark couverture chocolate, melted, slightly warm

3 oz (80 g) dark couverture chocolate, chopped

Granulated sugar

My dad loves the combination of orange and chocolate. When I opened my pastry shop, I created this chocolate and orange cookie just for him. My secret is to triple the amount of chocolate and always use the good stuff (it makes a difference!). These delicate and extremely chewy cookies are moist with a hint of crunch and the brightness of orange zest. This is a perfect pairing worthy of Dad.

1. In the bowl of a stand mixer fitted with the paddle attachment, cream together the brown sugar, butter, vanilla and orange zest until light and fluffy.

2. Add the eggs one at a time, mixing on low speed to combine each one before adding the next. Increase the speed to medium and continue creaming until the ingredients are fully incorporated.

3. In a separate bowl, sift together the flour, cocoa powder and baking soda. Add the salt.

4. With the mixer on low speed, slowly add the sifted ingredients to the butter mixture in thirds, scraping down the bowl before each addition. Add the warm melted chocolate and mix slowly until it is fully incorporated. Then add the chopped chocolate and mix just until fully incorporated.

5. Remove the dough from the bowl and roll it into 2 logs, each about 2 inches in diameter and 10 inches in length. Chill in the fridge for 45 minutes, so the logs hold their shape when slicing.

6. While the dough chills, preheat the oven to 325°F. Line a baking sheet with parchment paper.

7. Once the dough has chilled, slice each log into 20 pieces, each about 1 inch thick. The dough will still be a bit soft but should hold together.

8. Place some granulated sugar on a plate. Fully coat each cookie with sugar, then transfer to the lined baking sheet. Once all the cookies have been coated, bake them for 8 to 10 minutes. Remove from the oven and let cool on the baking sheet.

NOTE

You can freeze the cookie dough as logs, to slice from frozen and bake whenever you need a quick fix! They'll last in the freezer for up to 3 months or in the fridge for up to 1 week.

At the bakery I put the dough slices in little ring molds to help them keep their height while baking. If you bake them free-form, they'll flatten out but still taste just as delicious.

Salted Double Chocolate Chip Cookies

Makes 20 cookies

Prep Time: 10 minutes, plus 30 minutes for chilling

Cook Time: 12 to 15 minutes

¾ cup (175 g) unsalted butter, room temperature

½ cup + ⅓ cup (170 g) light brown sugar

¾ cup (150 g) granulated sugar

2 large eggs

3¼ teaspoons (10 g) vanilla extract

2⅓ cups (350 g) all-purpose flour

1 teaspoon baking soda

1 teaspoon kosher salt

3.6 oz (95 g) milk couverture chocolate, chopped

3.6 oz (95 g) semisweet dark couverture chocolate, chopped

Fleur de sel, for garnish

Chocolate chip cookies are beloved by everyone. I'm sure you have your own favorite recipe, but this one is worth trying. I like to use a combination of milk and semisweet chocolate, but you can kick it up a sophistication notch by using dark chocolate instead. At the end of the day, a chocolate chip cookie dipped in a glass of cold milk—or chocolate milk!—is the best thing in the world. (You'll find my recipe for chocolate milk on page 223.)

1. In the bowl of a stand mixer fitted with the paddle attachment, cream together the butter, brown sugar and granulated sugar on high speed, until light and fluffy, scraping down the bowl at least twice.

2. Reduce the speed to low and add the eggs one at a time. Add the vanilla. Continue beating on medium speed until fully incorporated, scraping down the bowl a few times.

3. In a separate bowl, sift together the flour and baking soda, then add the salt. Add to the butter mixture in thirds, beating on low speed until fully combined. Scrape down the bowl before each addition.

4. Add the chopped milk and semisweet chocolates and mix just to combine.

5. Remove the dough from the bowl and roll it into 2 logs, each about 2 inches in diameter and 10 inches in length. Chill the dough in the fridge for 30 minutes so the logs will hold their shape when slicing.

6. While the dough chills, preheat the oven to 325°F. Line a baking sheet with parchment paper.

7. When the dough is firm, remove it from the fridge and slice each log into 20 pieces, each about 1 inch thick.

8. Place the cookies on the baking sheet about 2 inches apart and sprinkle each with a little fleur de sel. Bake for 12 to 15 minutes. Remove from the oven and allow to cool on the sheet.

NOTE

You can freeze the cookie dough as logs, to slice from frozen and bake whenever you need a quick fix! They'll last in the freezer for up to 3 months or in the fridge for up to 1 week.

These cookies make fantastic ice-cream sandwiches using vanilla ice cream.

White Chocolate Peanut Butter Cookies

Makes 16 cookies

Prep Time: 20 minutes, plus 45 minutes for chilling

Cook Time: 15 to 17 minutes

⅓ cup + 2 tablespoons (105 g) unsalted butter, room temperature

⅓ cup + 1½ tablespoons (85 g) light brown sugar

⅓ cup (65 g) granulated sugar

½ cup (130 g) peanut butter

1 large egg

1¼ cups (190 g) all-purpose flour

1 teaspoon baking soda

1 teaspoon kosher salt

2 tablespoons (30 ml) whole milk

6.7 oz (190 g) white couverture chocolate, finely chopped

Granulated sugar

If I had to pick one ingredient to single out as a favorite (besides chocolate), it would be peanut butter, hands down. I eat peanut butter every day in some form. So it's probably no surprise that peanut butter cookies are my all-time favorite cookie. Adding white chocolate makes them a tad sweeter but also provides great texture and a hint of caramel, and it balances well with the nuttiness of the peanut butter.

1. In the bowl of a stand mixer fitted with the paddle attachment, cream together the butter, brown sugar and granulated sugar on medium speed, until fully incorporated, scraping down the bowl at least twice. Reduce the speed to low and add the peanut butter, mixing until fully combined. Add the egg and mix to combine.

2. Sift the flour into a separate bowl. Add the baking soda and salt.

3. In thirds, slowly add the dry ingredients to the butter mixture, beating on low speed to incorporate. Scrape down the bowl before each addition. Add the milk and mix at low speed to incorporate. Add the chopped white chocolate and mix just to combine.

4. Remove the cookie dough from the bowl. On parchment paper, roll it into 2 logs, each about 2 inches in diameter. Refrigerate for 45 minutes to set the dough.

5. While the dough chills, preheat the oven to 325°F. Line a baking sheet with parchment paper.

6. Remove the logs from the fridge and slice each into 10 equal pieces. Place some granulated sugar on a plate and dip the cookies in it to coat them fully. Place on the lined baking sheet at least 2 inches apart and bake for 15 to 17 minutes. Let cool completely on the baking sheet.

NOTE

Here's a little trick: three-quarters of the way through baking, press down the cookies with a fork. This will make them chewier.

Chocolate Almond Biscotti

Makes 15 cookies
Prep Time: 25 minutes
Cook Time: 1 hour, 40 minutes

½ cup (115 g) unsalted butter, room temperature

⅔ cup (140 g) granulated sugar

3 large eggs

1⅓ cups (200 g) all-purpose flour

⅓ cup (40 g) Dutch-process cocoa powder

1 tablespoon + 2 teaspoons (15 g) baking powder

¼ teaspoon kosher salt

1¾ cups (200 g) slivered almonds

8.6 oz (240 g) dark couverture chocolate

Biscotti cookies remind me of my time in Europe when I was a young pastry chef. I was working in London, England, going on no sleep, with no time to experience the city—just working 18 hours a day. On my way to work every day, I would grab a coffee or an espresso at a shop in Sloane Square before I jumped on the Tube, and it always came with a small biscotto. It was the highlight of my day, because I knew that for the rest of it I would be suffering in the kitchen. For me, these cookies are best served with coffee or tea.

1. In the bowl of a stand mixer fitted with the paddle attachment, cream together the butter and sugar on medium speed, until light and fluffy. Scrape down the bowl at least twice.

2. Slowly add the eggs, one at a time, mixing on medium speed to incorporate and scraping down the bowl as needed.

3. Sift together the flour, cocoa powder and baking powder into a bowl. Add the salt. Mixing on low speed, slowly add the dry ingredients to the butter mixture in thirds, scraping down the bowl before each addition.

4. Chop together the slivered almonds and chocolate. Add to the butter mixture and mix on low speed until fully combined.

5. Remove the dough from the bowl and place on a piece of parchment paper. Fold the paper over the dough to enclose it. Shape the dough into a biscotti log about 5½ inches wide and 16 inches long. Place the dough log, still in the parchment paper, in the fridge to set for 10 minutes.

6. Preheat the oven to 325°F. Line a baking sheet with parchment paper.

7. Remove the dough log from the fridge, unwrap it, and place it on the lined baking sheet. Bake the log for 40 minutes. Then remove from the oven and reduce the oven temperature to 180°F.

8. Let the log cool just enough to handle. Slice the par-baked dough into 15 pieces. Place back in the oven for 1 hour to dry out the biscotti. Because of the chocolate, it will be hard to tell when they're done. At 1 hour, remove a cookie to try the texture—if it's still chewy, keep baking. You can also check by looking at the almonds inside the cookie to see how dark they are getting; they should be a beautiful golden brown. Let the cookies cool completely on a wire rack before serving.

Peanut Butter Chocolate Energy Balls

Makes 12 balls
Prep Time: 30 minutes

---

20 pitted large dates

½ cup (50 g) unsweetened shredded coconut

½ cup (50 g) rolled oats

2½ tablespoons (20 g) hemp hearts

2¼ tablespoons (45 g) maple syrup

2 tablespoons (32 g) peanut butter

1 teaspoon cinnamon

½ teaspoon kosher salt

3 oz (80 g) bittersweet dark chocolate, chopped fine

These energy balls are a favorite in my household, and that's probably because they were created by my wife, Lara, who knows what everyone loves. They're a great go-to snack for kids and adults alike. These energy bites are moist, rich and super filling because of the protein from the peanut butter and the complex carbohydrates of the oats.

1. Combine the dates, coconut and oats in a food processor. Pulse until the mixture becomes almost like a paste. The broken-down dates will act as a binder for the rest of the ingredients.

2. Add the hemp hearts, maple syrup, peanut butter, cinnamon and salt. Pulse until combined.

3. Transfer the mixture to a large bowl and fold in the chocolate by hand. Portion into 12 equal amounts, then roll into balls. Store in the fridge until ready to eat.

NOTE

For an extra hit of chocolate, roll the balls in tempered chocolate, or garnish with chocolate shavings.

Chocolate Butter Shortbread

Makes 28 cookies

Prep Time: 25 minutes, plus 30 minutes for chilling

Cook Time: 8 to 10 minutes

---

²/₃ cup (150 g) unsalted butter, cold

½ cup (65 g) icing sugar

1 teaspoon vanilla extract

1 cup (150 g) all-purpose flour

1 tablespoon (8 g) Dutch-process cocoa powder

½ teaspoon kosher salt

7 oz (200 g) dark couverture chocolate, tempered

Like you, I imagine, I've eaten a lot of shortbread cookies during the holidays. But I've come to appreciate the mighty shortbread as more than a mere cookie. It can also serve as the base for a cake or as a crumble in parfaits. This crunchy cookie holds its structure for all those uses, as well as for eating with a glass of milk or a cup of tea. Now I find myself making this year-round. Adding dark chocolate creates a nice depth of flavor for variety.

1. In the bowl of a stand mixer fitted with the paddle attachment, cream together the butter, icing sugar and vanilla, until light and fluffy.

2. In a separate bowl, sift together the flour and cocoa powder, then add the salt.

3. Add the dry ingredients to the butter mixture and mix until the dough just comes together. Remove from the bowl. Form the dough into a square, wrap with plastic wrap and refrigerate for 30 minutes.

4. While the dough chills, preheat the oven to 325°F. Line a baking sheet with parchment paper.

5. Remove the dough from the fridge and lightly flour the dough and the work surface. Roll out the dough to about ¹/₈ inch thick. Use a 2-inch cookie cutter to cut out the cookies, then place them on the lined baking sheet.

6. Bake the cookies for 8 to 10 minutes, until light golden. Remember, the cookies will already look darker because of the chocolate, so be careful to watch for doneness. Remove from the oven and let cool completely.

7. Place the tempered chocolate in a bowl. Dip one-half of each cookie in the chocolate, or use a fork to drizzle some overtop. Set on a piece of parchment paper to cool.

Double Chocolate French Macarons

Makes 25 cookies
Prep Time: 1 hour
Cook Time: 10 to 15 minutes

Macarons

165 g almond flour

165 g icing sugar

5 g Dutch-process cocoa powder

4 large egg whites, divided

25 g + 140 g granulated sugar, divided

70 g water

Chocolate Ganache

215 g heavy cream

48 g corn syrup

9 oz (250 g) dark chocolate, chopped

30 g unsalted butter, room temperature

When making macarons, I'm of the belief that all the ingredients need to be weighed on a scale, not measured in cups—the ingredient ratios need to be precise. French macarons are delicate sandwich cookies. They have a thin, crisp shell on the outside but a surprisingly chewy center. They can be a bit tricky to make, but if you follow the process I've outlined here, you'll be in great shape. I like to use an Italian meringue because it has more structure and forms a firmer outer shell, without the need to rest the cookie.

1. For the macarons, place the almond flour and icing sugar in a food processor and blitz together to form a fine meal. Remove and place in a bowl, then add the cocoa powder and whisk to combine.

2. Sift the almond-flour mixture into a large bowl. Add 2 egg whites and mix together to form a paste.

3. Place the remaining 2 egg whites in the bowl of a stand mixer fitted with the whisk attachment. Whisk on the lowest speed until frothy. Add 25 g of granulated sugar, and whisk to soft peaks on medium speed.

4. Place the remaining 140 g of granulated sugar and the water in a pot set over medium heat. Using a candy thermometer, bring the mixture to soft-ball temperature, 245°F. Keep an eye on it—when the syrup reaches 239°F, turn the mixer speed to high and whip the egg whites to full volume. When the syrup hits 245°F, remove the pot from the stove, reduce the mixer speed to low, and slowly pour the syrup down the side of the bowl in a straight line. Once the syrup is fully added, increase the speed to high. Mix until the egg whites have fully cooled.

5. Place one-third of the egg whites in the bowl with the almond-flour paste and beat well using a silicone spatula. Fold in the remaining egg whites, beating well to remove all the air. Once the mixture is fully combined, you should have a consistency that spreads slightly when dropped back into the mixture.

6. Using 2 or 3 large pieces of parchment paper and a 1½-inch cookie cutter, trace 48 circles with a marker. Flip the parchment upside down to line 2 or 3 baking sheets.

Continued…

7. Fill a piping bag fitted with a ½-inch plain round tip with the batter. Holding the piping bag straight up, not at an angle, pipe the mixture into the middle and right to the edges of each circle on the parchment. Once all the macarons have been piped, give the baking sheets a quick bang on the counter to remove any air bubbles.

8. Preheat the oven to 300°F. Allow the sheets of macarons to dry out until they become pale in color and not sticky to touch, about 30 minutes. Bake for 10 to 15 minutes, until you can see the frilly "feet" form around the bottoms of the macarons. (You'll need to bake them in batches.)

9. To make the ganache filling, boil together the cream and corn syrup. Place the chocolate in a separate bowl. Once the cream has come to a boil, pour it over the chocolate. Emulsify with an immersion blender until the chocolate has melted and takes on a glossy finish.

10. Let the ganache sit until its temperature drops to 104°F, then emulsify the butter into the mixture with the immersion blender. Transfer the ganache into a piping bag with the same tip used to pipe the macarons.

11. Once the macarons have baked and cooled, flip them upside down on the baking sheets. Pipe the ganache onto half of the cookies and then sandwich the other halves onto them.

NOTE

Do not overmix the macaron batter, or it will become flat and won't produce "feet" at the bottoms of the macarons.

Creamy Dark Chocolate Ganache Cream Puffs

Makes 20 cream puffs
Prep Time: 1 hour, 30 minutes
Cook Time: 45 minutes

Craquelin

½ cup (115 g) unsalted butter, room temperature

½ cup (100 g) brown sugar

¾ cup (110 g) all-purpose flour

1 tablespoon (8 g) Dutch-process cocoa powder

Choux Pastry

1 cup (150 g) all-purpose flour

1½ tablespoons (12 g) Dutch-process cocoa powder

⅔ cup (150 g) unsalted butter, room temperature

½ cup + 2 tablespoons (155 ml) water

½ cup + 2 tablespoons (155 ml) whole milk

1 teaspoon kosher salt

1½ teaspoons granulated sugar

4 large eggs

Namelaka Chocolate Ganache

7 gelatin sheets or 4 teaspoons (14 g) gelatin powder

13.6 oz (385 g) dark couverture chocolate

1 cup (250 ml) whole milk

2 teaspoons corn syrup

2 cups (500 ml) heavy cream, cold

Choux pastry, also called pâte à choux, is a light, airy, crisp pastry. It forms the foundation of a great cream puff, as well as other desserts such as eclairs. I like to add a craquelin topping to make my cream puffs a little sweeter and crunchier. This dessert is served with a namelaka ganache, which is something I learned to make in Japan. *Namelaka* means "ultra-creamy," making it the perfect filling for cream puffs.

1. First start the craquelin. In the bowl of a stand mixer fitted with the paddle attachment, cream the butter and brown sugar. Add the flour and cocoa powder and mix to obtain a dough.

2. Roll out the craquelin dough between two pieces of parchment paper to about $\frac{1}{10}$ inch thick. Place in the freezer for 30 minutes.

3. Remove the dough from the freezer and cut out 20 circles, each 2½ inches in diameter. Return the circles to the freezer.

4. Preheat the oven to 370°F. Using a 2½-inch cookie cutter and a marker, draw 20 circles on sheets of parchment paper to use as guides when you pipe the choux. Flip over the paper and place it on as many baking sheets as are needed.

5. For the choux pastry, sift together the flour and cocoa powder into a bowl. Place the butter, water, milk, salt and sugar in a pot and bring the mixture to a boil, stirring to combine. Remove the pot from the heat and add the flour mixture. Mix with a wooden spoon to combine, then return the pot to medium heat. Stir for 2 minutes to create a dough that comes together and looks shiny.

6. Transfer the dough to the bowl of a stand mixer fitted with the paddle attachment. Mix on low speed until the dough cools to 113°F.

7. Slowly add the eggs, one at a time, making sure that each one is fully incorporated before adding the next. The dough is ready when you pinch it between your thumb and index finger and it's elastic. If the dough is too firm, add one more egg. (You may need an extra egg, or you may not need all of them.)

8. When the dough is ready, transfer it to a piping bag with a ½-inch round tip. Holding the piping bag straight up, pipe the dough onto the pre-marked circles.

Continued…

9. Place the craquelin circles on top of the choux circles and bake for 10 minutes. Then reduce the oven temperature to 350°F and bake for another 35 minutes. Do not open the oven or the choux pastry will collapse!

10. For the ganache, bloom the gelatin sheets in cold water. Once they are soft, strain out the excess water out and set aside. If using powdered gelatin, the ratio is 5 parts water to 1 part powdered gelatin.

11. Melt the chocolate in a bowl in the microwave (see page 7) and set aside.

12. Combine the milk and corn syrup in a small pot and bring it to a boil. Add the bloomed gelatin, then strain the mixture over the melted chocolate. Emulsify the mixture with a whisk or an immersion blender.

13. Immediately pour in the cold cream and whisk or blend to emulsify. Cover the ganache and refrigerate until firm, about 1 hour.

14. Once the ganache is firm, place it in a bowl of the stand mixer and whisk to lighten it to a pipeable consistency.

15. To assemble, cut the choux puffs in half horizontally. Fill a piping bag with the ganache and pipe the desired amount into the puffs. Place the tops, craquelin side up, over the ganache and eat.

NOTE

The namelaka ganache can be made the night before and kept in the fridge. You can also freeze the choux puffs after they are baked, if you decide not to pipe in the ganache.

Chocolate Canelés

Makes 12 canelés

Prep Time: 10 minutes, plus 24 hours for resting

Cook Time: 55 minutes

Canelés

1½ cups (375 ml) whole milk

1.6 oz (40 g) dark couverture chocolate, chopped

1 teaspoon vanilla extract

1½ cups (188 g) icing sugar

2 large eggs

2 large egg yolks

½ cup (75 g) all-purpose flour

2 tablespoons + ¼ cup (90 g) unsalted butter, melted, divided

5 teaspoons (25 ml) Grand Marnier

Simple Syrup

2 cups (400 g) granulated sugar

1 cup (250 ml) water

1 vanilla bean

When I started out my career, I worked at The Wolseley restaurant in London, England. It was there that I tried my first canelé—small and delicate, firm on the outside, gooey on the inside. It had the perfect balance of textures and flavors. That canelé became my go-to treat every day. Traditionally, canelé molds are coated in beeswax, but I use sugar to make them a little sweeter and give them a firmer crust.

1. For the canelés, heat the milk, chocolate and vanilla in a small pot set over medium heat until the chocolate melts fully.

2. Cool the mixture to room temperature, then add the icing sugar, eggs, egg yolks, flour, 2 tablespoons of melted butter and Grand Marnier. Use a handheld mixer or immersion blender to fully incorporate the ingredients.

3. Strain the mixture through a fine sieve into a plastic container and cover with plastic wrap or a lid. Allow the mixture to rest in the fridge for 24 hours.

4. To make the simple syrup, place the sugar and water in a pot. Scrape the vanilla bean and add the seeds to the pot. Bring to a boil, then remove from the heat. Transfer to a container and place it in the fridge until you are ready to use the syrup.

5. When ready to bake, preheat the oven to 375°F. Whisk the simple syrup to reincorporate it, as it will separate in the fridge.

6. To coat the canelé molds, brush the inside of each mold with the remaining ¼ cup melted butter, then sprinkle granulated sugar inside to coat the entire mold. Knock out any excess sugar, then carefully fill the mold with the canelé mixture to ¼ inch below the rim.

7. Place the canelés in the oven and bake for 25 minutes. Then reduce the temperature to 325°F and bake for another 25 to 30 minutes. The mixture should be slightly raised to the rim and not jiggly in the middle.

8. Allow the canelés to cool for 5 minutes, then remove from the molds. Dip each canelé in simple syrup, then enjoy.

NOTE

You need to pre-make the batter and allow it to sit for 24 hours. This relaxes the batter and releases air bubbles, which will ensure a denser canelé. If the batter does not rest, it will puff up too much when baked. Traditionally canelés are baked in copper molds lined with beeswax, but you can use silicone or Teflon-coated molds as well.

Whoopie Pies

Makes 8 sandwich cookies
Prep Time: 45 minutes
Cook Time: 10 to 12 minutes

Whoopie Pies

1½ cups + 1½ tablespoons (240 g) all-purpose flour

½ cup (60 g) natural cocoa powder

¾ teaspoon baking soda

¼ teaspoon baking powder

½ teaspoon kosher salt

1 cup (250 ml) buttermilk

2 teaspoons vanilla extract

½ cup (115 g) unsalted butter, room temperature

¾ cup (150 g) granulated sugar

¼ cup (50 g) dark brown sugar

1 large egg

Chocolate Buttercream

3 large egg whites

1 cup (200 g) granulated sugar

3 tablespoons (45 ml) water

1⅓ cups (300 g) unsalted butter, room temperature

2.8 oz (80 g) dark couverture chocolate, melted

The whoopie pie is a classic American sandwich cookie. But there aren't really any cookies to be found here—the sandwich parts are more like small cakes than anything else. The filling is traditionally a rich and delicious buttercream, but you can also use a mousse, a ganache or even a fruit preserve. These are the perfect afternoon snacks that everyone will love.

1. Preheat the oven to 350°F. Line 2 baking sheets with parchment paper.

2. For the whoopie pies, sift together the flour, cocoa powder, baking soda and baking powder into a large bowl, then add the salt. In a separate bowl, whisk together the buttermilk and vanilla.

3. In the bowl of a stand mixer fitted with the paddle attachment, cream together the butter, granulated sugar and brown sugar until light and fluffy. Add the egg and combine fully.

4. Alternately add the flour mixture and buttermilk mixture to the butter mixture, beginning and ending with the dry ingredients.

5. Using a #20 yellow (1½ oz) ice-cream scoop, portion out 16 whoopie pies on the lined baking sheets. Bake for 10 to 12 minutes, until the cakes are dry to the touch but spring back when lightly poked. You'll likely need to bake them in batches.

6. For the buttercream, place the egg whites in a bowl of the stand mixer fitted with the paddle attachment, and start mixing on low speed.

7. Combine the sugar and water in a pot and cook over medium heat until the temperature reaches 245°F. Remove the pot from the heat and allow the bubbles to deflate.

8. Increase the speed of the mixer and whisk the egg whites to full volume.

9. Reduce the mixer speed to the lowest setting and slowly pour the sugar syrup down the side of the bowl in a straight line. Once it has been added, increase the speed to the highest setting and whisk until the egg whites have fully cooled down and come to full volume.

10. Slowly add the butter, a little bit at a time, mixing until the mixture is fully emulsified and looks like buttercream.

11. Melt the chocolate in the microwave (see page 7). Stir the melted chocolate into the buttercream. Scrape down the sides and bottom of the bowl to make sure the chocolate is fully incorporated.

12. To assemble the whoopie pies, place the buttercream in a piping bag or use a #30 black (1 ounce) ice-cream scoop. Flip half of the cakes upside down on a baking sheet, pipe or scoop some filling onto the bottoms, and then sandwich together. Store whoopie pies in the fridge for a moist treat.

Dark Chocolate Butter Tarts

Makes 17 to 18 tarts
Prep Time: 1 hour
Cook Time: 20 to 25 minutes

Brisée Dough

1½ cups (340 g) unsalted butter, cold

1¾ cups + 4 teaspoons (282 g) all-purpose flour

1 tablespoon (10 g) kosher salt

⅓ cup (75 ml) cold water

Filling

6.7 oz (190 g) dark couverture chocolate

⅔ cup (132 g) dark brown sugar

¼ cup (60 g) unsalted butter, room temperature

¾ teaspoon vanilla extract

¼ teaspoon kosher salt

2 large eggs

3 tablespoons (45 ml) heavy cream

6½ tablespoons (100 ml) maple syrup

½ cup (80 g) raisins

If you have never had a classic butter tart, this recipe is a must-try. It hits all the taste buds, and it's so easy to make. These tarts are unbelievably gooey, buttery and flaky—a perfect treat for those with a sweet tooth. I like to use a French brisée dough for a buttery, flaky pastry, but regular pie dough is fine as well. You'll see that I use raisins, but if you're not a fan, try pecans (or nothing) in the filling.

1. For the dough, place the butter in the freezer for 10 minutes to firm up. Then grate the butter into a bowl and place in the fridge while you measure the other ingredients.

2. Combine the flour and salt in a food processor. Add the chilled grated butter. Pulse for a few seconds and then add the water. Continue to pulse until the dough comes together slightly. Remove from the food processor and hand-knead to bring it all together. Do not overwork the dough; it's okay if some of it flakes off. Pat the dough into a square about 2 inches thick. Wrap with plastic wrap and place in the fridge to relax for 30 minutes.

3. While the dough is relaxing, start the tart filling. Preheat the oven to 350°F.

4. Melt the chocolate in a microwave (see page 7) and set aside. In the bowl of a stand mixer fitted with the paddle attachment, cream together the brown sugar, butter, vanilla and salt, until light and fluffy.

5. Beat in the eggs, then the cream and maple syrup, followed by the raisins. Add the melted chocolate and stir to fully combine. Set aside in the fridge until you are ready to use.

6. Take the brisée dough out of the fridge and lightly dust the dough and your work surface with flour. Roll out the dough to $^{1}/_{10}$ inch thick. Using a 4½-inch cookie cutter, cut out rounds.

7. Spray a standard-sized muffin tin with nonstick spray, then line the wells with the brisée rounds. Leave about ¼ inch of dough above the rim. Place the muffin tin in the freezer for 10 minutes to relax the dough, so it does not shrink when baking.

8. Take the filling out of the fridge and give it a stir to reincorporate. Remove the lined muffin tin from the freezer and fill the tarts, using a 1-ounce ladle or #30 black (1 ounce) ice-cream scoop.

9. Bake the tarts in the preheated oven for 20 minutes. Let cool completely, then remove from the muffin tin.

NOTE

The filling can keep for up to 1 week in the fridge. It will separate as it sits, so before using it, always give the mixture a good stir.

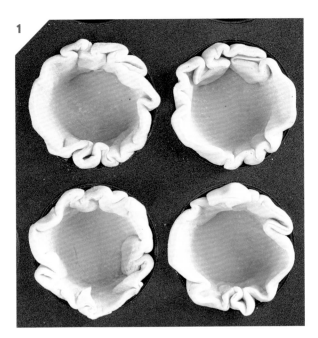

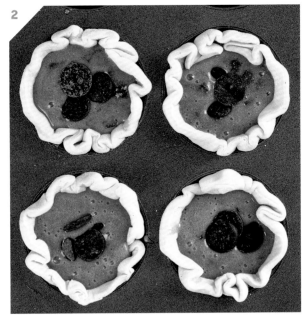

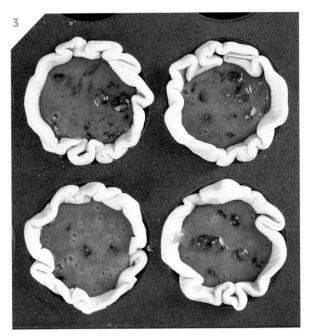

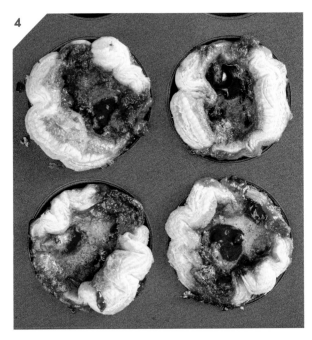

Steve's Sandwich Cookies

Makes 25 sandwich cookies
Prep Time: 1 hour, 15 minutes
Cook Time: 6 minutes

Cookie Dough

½ cup (115 g) unsalted butter, room temperature

½ cup (100 g) granulated sugar

¼ cup (50 g) dark brown sugar

1 teaspoon vanilla extract

¾ cup + 1 tablespoon (125 g) all-purpose flour

¼ cup (30 g) Dutch-process cocoa powder

½ teaspoon kosher salt

1 large egg

Icing

3.5 oz (100 g) white couverture chocolate

1 cup + 2½ tablespoons (150 g) icing sugar

¼ cup (60 g) cream cheese

1 tablespoon (14 g) unsalted butter, room temperature

1½ teaspoons vanilla extract

I dreamed up these treats when I was a young chef working at a restaurant in Hollywood called Dominick's. The chef asked me to create an ice-cream sandwich. As I worked on the cookie part of the recipe, I tested it by making sandwiches using icing I had made earlier for a carrot cake. I admit I ate quite a few in the interest of getting the recipe just right. The next day I sandwiched my cookies with the cream cheese icing, and the chef added it to the menu that night. I still often get requests to make them.

1. For the cookie dough, combine the butter, granulated sugar, brown sugar and vanilla in the bowl of a stand mixer fitted with the paddle attachment. Cream on high speed until light and fluffy, scraping down the bowl a few times.

2. In a separate bowl, sift together the flour and cocoa powder. Add the salt.

3. With the mixer on low speed, add the egg to the butter mixture and cream until fully incorporated. Give the bowl a scrape to make sure nothing sticks.

4. Still beating on low speed, add the dry ingredients in thirds, scraping the bowl after each addition.

5. Remove the dough from the bowl and form a flat square. Wrap with plastic wrap and place in the fridge for 1 hour. Halfway through the chilling time, preheat the oven to 325°F. Line 2 baking sheets with parchment paper.

6. For the icing, melt the white chocolate in the microwave (see page 7) and set aside. Combine the icing sugar, cream cheese, butter and vanilla in the bowl of the stand mixer fitted with the paddle attachment. Beat until light and fluffy. Then add the melted chocolate and beat to combine. Cover the bowl with plastic wrap and set aside in the fridge.

7. Remove the dough from the fridge and flour your work surface. Roll out the dough to $1/8$ inch thick and cut out circles 2 inches in diameter.

8. Place the cut-out cookies on the lined baking sheets and bake for 4 minutes. Allow to cool completely.

9. Flip half of the baked cookies upside down and fill a piping bag with the icing. Pipe about 1½ teaspoons of frosting on each bottom half, then sandwich the cookies together. Store the cookies in the fridge in an airtight container. These are soft and chewy, so they are best served cold, right from the fridge.

Chocolate Rum Babas

Makes 14 babas

Prep Time: 30 minutes, plus 1 hour, 30 minutes for proofing

Cook Time: 20 minutes

Chocolate Babas

½ cup (125 ml) whole milk

4 teaspoons (12 g) active dry yeast

3 large eggs

2½ cups (375 g) all-purpose flour

2 tablespoons (15 g) Dutch-process cocoa powder

2 tablespoons (25 g) granulated sugar

½ teaspoon kosher salt

½ cup (115 g) unsalted butter, room temperature

Chocolate Rum Soak

2 cups (400 g) granulated sugar

2 cups (500 ml) water

1 cup (250 ml) rum

½ cup (125 ml) chocolate liqueur

Whipped Cream

1 cup (250 ml) heavy cream

1 tablespoon (8 g) icing sugar

1 teaspoon Dutch-process cocoa powder

How would I sum up this dessert? Moist, sweet, soft and full of rum flavor. These little yeast cakes, called rum babas or babas au rhum, are baked in single-serving molds, then soaked in a rum syrup. They are usually served with a dollop of whipped cream and fresh fruit. Rum baba is well loved in our household, whether we're hosting a dinner party or a birthday event.

1. To make the babas, first warm the milk for 30 seconds in the microwave. Dissolve the yeast in the warm milk and let sit for 5 minutes to get frothy. Then whisk the eggs into the mixture.

2. In the bowl of a stand mixer fitted with the dough hook, combine the flour, cocoa powder, sugar and salt. Add the milk-and-egg mixture and mix on low speed. When the dough starts to look like crumbs, add the butter, bit by bit. When completely added, increase the speed to medium. Mix the dough until it comes together and looks sticky and soft, about 5 minutes.

3. Transfer the dough to a floured work surface and cover with plastic wrap. Proof the dough until doubled in size, about 1 hour.

4. Grease the baba molds. Divide the dough into 2-ounce (portions, the size of golf balls. Place a portion in each mold and proof for another 30 minutes, covered with plastic.

5. During the second proof, preheat the oven to 350°F.

6. Bake the babas for 20 minutes. Remove from the molds and transfer to a wire rack to cool.

7. For the soak, boil together the sugar and water. Add the rum and the chocolate liqueur and mix well. Remove from the heat.

8. Prick the top and bottom of each baba with a toothpick, then submerge in the syrup for 30 seconds. Place the babas on a wire rack and let them absorb the syrup. You can also place the babas in a jar and top them with the liquid, as in the photo, for a more moist version.

9. For the whipped cream, combine the cream, icing sugar and cocoa powder in a bowl. Whisk to soft peaks.

10. To serve, transfer the babas to a serving dish, then dollop a spoonful of whipped cream on each rum baba.

NOTE

If you like, you can grate some dark chocolate or create chocolate curls to serve overtop the finished babas (see page 13).

Frozen

Creamy Double Chocolate Ice Cream

Makes about 1 quart (950 ml)
Prep Time: 10 minutes, plus 1 hour chilling
Cook Time: 5 minutes

1¼ oz (50 g) dark chocolate

2 tablespoons (40 g) corn syrup

1½ cups (375 ml) heavy cream

1 cup (250 ml) whole milk

1 teaspoon vanilla extract

¾ cup (142 g) granulated sugar

3 large egg yolks

¼ cup + 2 teaspoons (35 g) Dutch-process cocoa powder

Dark chocolate curls (see page 13), for garnish

Homemade ice cream is creamy, silky and full of flavor. If you have the right equipment, it's also easy and fun to make. I use a professional machine to churn ice creams in my shop, but there are many inexpensive options on the market that do a great job. I've given you a few recipes in this book to help start building up your freezer inventory.

1. Finely chop the chocolate. Place it in a large bowl, along with the corn syrup. Set aside.

2. In a pot, combine the cream, milk and vanilla. Bring to a boil over medium-high heat and set aside.

3. Whisk together the sugar and egg yolks in a large bowl. Temper the eggs by pouring in half of the hot cream mixture and whisking together. Transfer to the pot with the remaining cream mixture, whisking to combine.

4. Whisk in the cocoa powder and place the pot over medium heat. Cook for 3 to 5 minutes, whisking continuously, until the mixture becomes thick enough to coat the back of a spoon. If you're using a thermometer, it should read about 180°F when inserted into the mixture.

5. Prepare an ice bath and set aside.

6. Strain the mixture over the chocolate and corn syrup. Whisk until the mixture is smooth and the chocolate fully melted.

7. Immediately place the bowl in the ice bath to cool down the mixture, stirring constantly. Once it is cool, place the bowl in the fridge for 1 hour to chill completely.

8. Churn into ice cream according to your machine's directions.

Milk Chocolate Ice Cream

Makes just over 1 quart (1.3 L)
Prep Time: 10 minutes
Cook Time: 5 minutes

---

2 tablespoons (15 g) Dutch-process cocoa powder

5.2 oz (150 g) milk chocolate

1 tablespoon (20 g) corn syrup

3¼ cups (810 ml) whole milk

1¼ cups (310 ml) heavy cream

7 egg yolks

¾ cup + 1½ tablespoons (166 g) granulated sugar

I love milk chocolate ice cream, because it reminds me of eating a chocolate bar. Milk chocolate has great flavor notes of milk and caramel; it's also rich in texture and velvety to the taste. This ice cream is smooth and melts immediately in your mouth. This is the perfect canvas for adding roasted fruits, nuts, caramel or even just a dollop of whipped cream.

1. Sift the cocoa powder into a medium pot and set aside.

2. Finely chop the chocolate. Place it in a large bowl along with the corn syrup. Set aside.

3. Pour the milk and cream into the pot with the cocoa powder. Bring to a boil over medium-high heat, whisking to incorporate the cocoa powder. Set aside.

4. Whisk together the egg yolks and sugar in a large bowl. Temper the eggs by pouring in half of the warm milk mixture and whisking together. Transfer to the pot with the remaining milk mixture, whisking to combine.

5. Place the pot over medium heat. Cook for 3 to 5 minutes, whisking continuously, until the mixture becomes thick enough to coat the back of a spoon. If you're using a thermometer, it should read about 180°F when inserted into the mixture.

6. Prepare an ice bath and set aside.

7. Strain the mixture over the chocolate and corn syrup. Whisk until the mixture is smooth and the chocolate fully melted.

8. Immediately place the bowl in the ice bath to cool down the mixture, stirring constantly. Once it is cool, place the bowl in the fridge for 1 hour to chill completely.

9. Churn into ice cream according to your machine's directions.

Ruby Chocolate Ice Cream

Makes 1½ quarts (1½ L)
Prep Time: 10 minutes
Cook Time: 5 minutes

---

15 oz (426 g) ruby chocolate chips
¼ cup (85 g) corn syrup
2 cups (500 ml) heavy cream
1 cup (250 ml) whole milk
6 large egg yolks
1 cup (200 g) granulated sugar
2 oz (60 g) raspberry purée, cold

Ruby is the newest of chocolates. It has fruity and acidic notes, which makes it a refreshing summer option to pair with raspberries or lemons. For an added hit of flavor, swirl in your favorite fruit purée right before you churn the ice cream.

1. Place the chocolate chips and corn syrup in a bowl. Set aside.

2. In a pot, combine the cream and milk. Bring to a boil over medium-high heat. Set aside.

3. In a separate bowl, whisk together the egg yolks and sugar.

4. Temper the eggs by whisking in half of the hot cream mixture, then transfer to the pot with the remaining cream mixture. Place the pot over low heat and cook, stirring constantly, until the mixture becomes thick enough to coat the back of a spoon. If you're using a thermometer, it should read about 180°F when inserted into the mixture.

5. Strain the custard over the chocolate and corn syrup, whisking to emulsify and melt the chocolate.

6. Prepare an ice bath and set aside.

7. Immediately place the bowl in an ice bath to cool down the mixture, stirring constantly. Once it is cool, place the bowl in the fridge for 1 hour to chill completely.

8. When the custard base has chilled, transfer it to your ice-cream machine, pour in the raspberry purée and churn according to your machine's directions. Freeze or enjoy right away!

White Chocolate Ice Cream

Makes about 1 quart (1.1 L)
Prep Time: 10 minutes
Cook Time: 5 minutes

---

7 oz (200 g) white chocolate

3 tablespoons (60 g) corn syrup

6 large egg yolks

½ cup + ⅓ cup (165 g) granulated
  sugar

1¾ cups (425 ml) whole milk

1 cup (250 ml) heavy cream

In my house we all scream for the sweet creaminess of this full-bodied ice cream. I love using white chocolate in ice cream. It creates a flavor that is similar to vanilla, but it's creamier because of the added fat from the chocolate. This ice cream works well with all kinds of flavors, so mix it up with different toppings.

1. Chop the chocolate and place it in a bowl with the corn syrup. Set aside.

2. In a separate bowl, whisk together the egg yolks and sugar.

3. In a pot, combine the milk and cream. Bring to a boil over medium-high heat.

4. Temper the egg yolks by pouring in half the hot milk mixture, whisking continuously. Then transfer the mixture to the pot with the remaining milk.

5. Place the pot over medium heat. Whisk constantly to thicken the custard until it coats the back of a spoon. If you're using a thermometer, it should reach 180°F.

6. Prepare an ice bath and set aside.

7. Remove the pot from the heat. Strain the custard over the chocolate and corn syrup, whisking constantly to emulsify and melt the chocolate. Place the bowl in an ice bath to cool, whisking constantly. Once it is cooled, transfer to the fridge to chill for 1 hour.

8. Churn into ice cream according to your machine's directions. This ice cream is best served as soon as it's churned.

Chocolate Sorbet

Makes 1 quart (1 L)
Prep Time: 5 minutes
Cook Time: 3 minutes

3½ cups (875 ml) water

1 cup + 1 tablespoon (210 g) granulated sugar

½ cup (60 g) Dutch-process cocoa powder

3 oz (80 g) dark chocolate

1 tablespoon (20 g) corn syrup

Sorbet is a frozen dessert made from sugar, water and flavoring. This is a refreshing dessert to serve after a heavy meal. Cocoa powder creates a bitter note, but because of the water and sugar content, it balances beautifully and it's a great alternative as a dairy-free dessert.

1. In a large pot, combine the water, sugar and cocoa powder. Bring to a boil.

2. Chop the chocolate and place it in a bowl along with the corn syrup. Pour the hot mixture into the bowl. Using an immersion blender, emulsify the mixture to create a smooth consistency.

3. Strain the mixture into a clean container. Set it in the fridge until fully cooled (it's best to leave it in the fridge overnight).

4. Place the chilled sorbet mixture in an ice-cream machine and churn.

NOTE

This sorbet is best served right after it has been churned.

Chocolate Neapolitan Roasted Banana Splits

Makes 2 banana splits
Prep Time: 10 minutes
Cook Time: 30 minutes

Strawberry Compote

1 cup (160 g) frozen strawberries

3 tablespoons (45 ml) water

1 tablespoon (15 g) granulated sugar

¼ cup pineapple chunks

2 large bananas

4 tablespoons (60 g) granulated sugar

¼ cup (28 g) peanuts

2 scoops Creamy Double Chocolate Ice Cream (page 169 or store-bought)

2 scoops Ruby Chocolate Ice Cream (page 173)

2 scoops White Chocolate Ice Cream (page 174)

¼ cup (60 ml) Chocolate Sauce (page 238 or store-bought)

Whipped Cream

1 cup (250 ml) heavy cream

1 tablespoon (8 g) icing sugar

Optional Toppings

Maraschino cherries

Fresh strawberries

Instead of the traditional strawberry, chocolate and vanilla ice cream banana split, I like to change it up with a dark, ruby and white chocolate ice-cream version. Incorporating caramelized bananas takes this old-school dessert into exciting new territory. This dessert makes Friday movie night on the couch a little more interesting.

1. Preheat the oven to 325°F. Line 2 baking sheets with parchment paper.

2. For the strawberry compote, combine the strawberries, water and sugar in a pot. Place over medium heat and bring to a boil. Then reduce the heat to low and simmer for 10 minutes to thicken the mixture. Continue to stir, then remove from the heat and pour onto an unlined baking sheet to cool.

3. Place the pineapple chunks on a lined baking sheet and roast in the preheated oven for 10 minutes.

4. Slice the bananas in half lengthwise. Sprinkle 1 tablespoon sugar evenly over the cut sides of each banana. Place on a lined baking sheet and caramelize in the oven on broil, for 3 to 5 minutes. If you have a kitchen blowtorch, you can brûlée the sugar on the banana instead.

5. Place the peanuts in a dry sauté pan over medium heat and toast them for 5 minutes, continually moving the nuts around the pan. Once they are golden, transfer to a wide-mouthed bowl. With the bottom of a cup or the end of a rolling pin, crush the nuts to a coarse consistency.

6. For the whipped cream, combine the cream and icing sugar and whisk to soft peaks. Set aside in the fridge until assembly.

7. To assemble, place 1 scoop of each flavor of ice cream in each banana split dish. Place a half banana lengthwise on each side of the ice cream. Pour the chocolate sauce all over the ice cream. Evenly distribute the pineapple and strawberry compote overtop. Dollop whipped cream over each scoop of ice cream. Finally, sprinkle the crushed peanuts all over, and top with cherries and strawberries, if using.

Chocolate Affogato

Makes one 6-ounce cup

Prep Time: 5 minutes

---

2 oz scoop Creamy Double
  Chocolate Ice Cream (page 169,
  or store-bought)

2 oz fresh espresso

This is the perfect pick-me-up after dinner. An affogato is traditionally a scoop of vanilla ice cream with espresso poured overtop. Don't get me wrong—I love coffee and I love vanilla ice cream, but chocolate ice cream makes this a little richer and more indulgent.

1. Using a #16 blue (2 oz) ice-cream scoop, place 1 scoop of ice cream in a cup. Pour the espresso overtop and enjoy.

Chocolate Chunk Peppermint Ice-Cream Bars

Makes 12 bars

Prep Time: 10 minutes, plus 30 minutes for chilling

Cook Time: 5 minutes

Ice Cream

1¼ cups (300 ml) whole milk

¾ cup + 5 teaspoons (200 ml) heavy cream

1 vanilla bean, scraped

5 large egg yolks

½ cup (100 g) granulated sugar

1 tablespoon (24 g) corn syrup

1½ teaspoons peppermint extract

3 oz (80 g) bittersweet dark chocolate, finely chopped

Chocolate Coating

14 oz (400 g) dark chocolate

¾ cup + 5 teaspoons (200 ml) coconut oil or vegetable oil

I've always loved the refreshing quality of peppermint ice cream. Adding chopped chocolate gives it texture and a bittersweet flavor element that balances the strong peppermint. Coating these bars in chocolate incorporates some chew while delivering even more flavor. You'll need some silicone ice-cream bar molds and popsicle sticks for this recipe.

1. For the ice cream, combine the milk, cream and vanilla bean seeds and pod in a medium pot. Bring to a boil over medium-high heat, then remove the pot from the heat and set aside.

2. In a separate bowl, whisk together the egg yolks and sugar to combine.

3. Temper the eggs by adding half of the milk mixture. Whisk together, then pour into the pot with the remaining milk.

4. Place the pot back on the stove over medium heat and cook for 2 to 3 minutes, whisking continuously, until the mixture is thick enough to coat the back of a spoon. If you're using a thermometer, the temperature should read 180°F when inserted into the mixture. Stir the mixture constantly so it doesn't burn or scramble.

5. Once the custard has thickened, remove the pot from the heat. Place the corn syrup in a large bowl with a fine-mesh strainer set overtop. Strain the custard into the bowl, then whisk in the peppermint extract. If you want a stronger peppermint flavor, add a little more, but go slowly so you don't overdo it.

6. Prepare an ice bath and place the custard bowl in it to cool. Then transfer the bowl to the fridge for about 30 minutes to chill.

7. When you're ready to make the ice cream, add the finely chopped chocolate to the custard and then churn the ice cream until set. You want it to be slightly malleable, though, so you can get it into the molds.

8. Remove the ice cream from the machine, transfer it to ice-cream bar molds, and insert popsicle sticks lengthwise through the center. Freeze until fully set.

9. To prepare the coating, melt the chocolate in the microwave (see page 7), then whisk in the oil. Set aside. For dipping the ice-cream bars, the coating mixture should be fully melted and at 90°F.

10. When the ice-cream bars are fully frozen, remove from the molds and dip into the chocolate coating. Place the dipped bars on a baking sheet lined with parchment paper. Freeze until the chocolate has set, about 30 minutes, and enjoy.

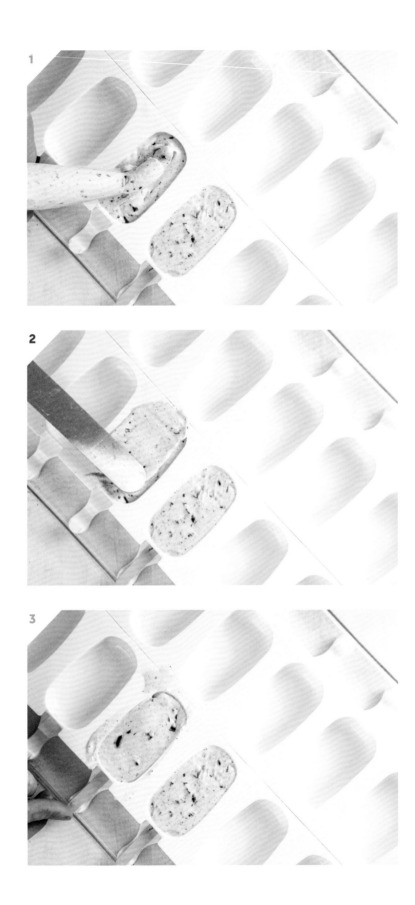

Chocolate Chunk Ice-Cream Sandwiches

Makes 16 sandwiches
Prep Time: 45 minutes
Cook Time: 20 minutes

Chocolate Chunk Ice Cream

⅓ cup (50 g) Creamy Double Chocolate Ice Cream (page 169, or store-bought)

5 oz (150 g) coarsely chopped dark chocolate

Almond Chocolate Shortbread Cookies

2¼ cups (340 g) all-purpose flour

½ cup (56 g) almond flour

2 tablespoons (15 g) Dutch-process cocoa powder

Pinch salt

1½ cups (340 g) unsalted butter

1⅓ cups (170 g) icing sugar

2 egg yolks

The ice-cream sandwich is the ultimate summer treat. I remember as a kid going to a corner store called Harry's Market, right down the street from where I lived. It was like *Groundhog Day* every time I walked in—straight to the back to grab a classic rectangular ice-cream sandwich from the freezer. I love the fact that you can use any type of cookie to put these together. Whether you like soft, chewy or crunchy cookies, the options are endless. Try out the recipes in this book to find your own signature ice-cream sandwich cookie. Have fun and change up the ice cream too.

1. Prepare the ice cream as instructed on page 169. Add the chopped dark chocolate to the base when churning the ice cream, and freeze as per the recipe.

2. To make the cookies, sift together the all-purpose flour, almond flour, cocoa powder, and salt in a large bowl. Whisk to combine and set aside.

3. In the bowl of a stand mixer fitted with the paddle attachment, cream the butter and icing sugar on high speed until light and fluffy, about 4 minutes.

4. Reduce the mixer speed to low and add the egg yolks one at a time, beating until incorporated, and scraping the bowl between additions. Increase the speed to high and beat for another 30 seconds.

5. Reduce the speed to low and slowly add the flour mixture. Be careful not to overwork the dough. As soon as it comes together, stop mixing.

6. Remove the dough from the bowl and place on a floured work surface. Bring the dough together to create a square, then wrap in plastic wrap and place in the fridge for 30 minutes.

7. While the dough is resting, line a baking sheet with parchment paper and place an 8-inch square cake frame (with no bottom) on the paper. Spread the ice cream evenly inside the frame to about 1½ to 2 inches deep. Place in the freezer to set fully.

8. Preheat the oven to 325°F. Line another baking sheet with parchment paper.

Continued…

9. Take the dough out of the fridge and flour your work surface. Roll out the dough to between $^1/_{16}$ and $^1/_8$ inch thick. Cut out rounds with a 3-inch round cookie cutter. Re-form the excess dough into a ball and roll out again to make more cookies, or wrap it in plastic wrap and place in the freezer for another time.

10. Place the cookies on the baking sheet, 1 inch apart (you'll need to bake them in batches). Bake for 8 to 10 minutes, until they become dull looking. Remove from the oven and let cool on a wire rack.

11. Once the ice cream is firmly set, use the 3-inch cookie cutter to cut out ice-cream rounds. Save any leftover ice cream for a cook's treat!

12. Sandwich together the cooled cookies and the ice-cream rounds. You can return them to the freezer, wrapped well in parchment paper, or enjoy them immediately.

The Ultimate Crunchy Chocolate Sundae

Makes 3 sundaes
Prep Time: 2 hours
Cook Time: 25 minutes

Creamy Double Chocolate Ice Cream (page 169, or store-bought)

Cherry Compote

500 g fresh pitted sweet cherries, frozen

½ orange, zested

3 tablespoons (45 ml) water

1 tablespoon (8 g) cornstarch

Pinch ground cinnamon

½ batch Hot Fudge Sauce (page 237)

Candied Almonds

½ cup (125 ml) water

½ cup (100 g) granulated sugar

1 cup (100 g) slivered or sliced almonds

Speculoos Crunch

1 cup (225 g) unsalted butter, room temperature

½ cup (100 g) brown sugar

¼ cup (50 g) granulated sugar

3¾ cups (420 g) all-purpose flour

2 teaspoons ground cinnamon

2 teaspoons baking powder

½ teaspoon kosher salt

1 large egg

2 tablespoons (30 ml) whole milk

9 oz (250 g) dark couverture chocolate, melted

Whipped Cream

1 cup (250 ml) heavy cream

2 tablespoons (16 g) icing sugar

A lot of frozen desserts bring back great memories for me, and now I try to create the same great memories for my kids. Ordering a sundae at the local ice-cream shop was a real treat. Because it had everything on it, it felt like you were getting more than just one dessert. The hot sauce, the crunch from the nuts, the freshness of the fruit and the cooling creaminess of the ice cream hit every sensation in the mouth, which is probably why it's so memorable for me and for countless others.

1. If you're making the ice cream from scratch, start that first.

2. For the compote, combine the frozen cherries, orange zest and water in a pot. In a separate bowl, whisk together the cornstarch and cinnamon.

3. Place the pot over medium heat and bring to a simmer. Once simmering, add the cornstarch mixture and increase the heat to medium-high. Using a spatula, stir the mixture to combine it fully and allow it to come to a boil. Keep stirring so the mixture doesn't burn to the bottom of the pot, and boil for 2 minutes, until thickened. Spread the mixture on a baking sheet to cool. Place in the fridge to chill.

4. To candy the almonds, preheat the oven to 325°F. Line a baking sheet with parchment paper. Combine the water and sugar in a pot and bring to a boil.

5. Place the almonds in a bowl and pour the hot sugar syrup over them. Mix with a spatula to fully coat the almonds. Strain the nuts to remove excess syrup and spread them on the lined baking sheet.

6. Bake the almonds for 5 minutes. Using the spatula, stir and turn the almonds on the baking sheet. Bake for another 5 minutes, then mix them again. Bake for another 2 minutes. The almonds should be evenly roasted and have a powdery white coating from the crystalized sugar. Remove from the oven and cool. Set aside.

7. Make the Hot Fudge Sauce (page 237) or use store-bought sauce.

8. For the speculoos, in the bowl of a stand mixer fitted with the paddle attachment, cream together the butter, brown sugar and granulated sugar on medium speed, until light and fluffy.

Continued…

9. In a separate bowl sift together the flour, cinnamon, baking powder and salt.

10. Reduce the mixer speed to low. Add the egg and milk to the butter mixture and mix until fully incorporated. Increase the speed to medium and beat for 1 minute.

11. Slowly add the dry ingredients and mix until a dough forms.

12. Shape the dough into a flat square. Wrap with plastic wrap and chill in the fridge for 1 hour.

13. While the dough chills, line a baking sheet with parchment paper. When the dough is firm enough to roll out, flour your work surface and roll out the dough to about $^3/_8$ inch thick. Place the rolled-out dough on the lined baking sheet and bake for 10 minutes, until crunchy and a light golden color. Remove from the oven and let cool on a wire rack.

14. Break up the cookie into pieces small enough to fit easily into the food processor. Pulse until you achieve a medium-coarse texture.

15. Melt the chocolate in the microwave. Place the cookie crumbs in a bowl. Pour in the melted chocolate and mix with a spatula to coat. Pour onto a baking sheet lined with parchment paper and spread out evenly. Allow the chocolate to set, then break up the pieces with your hands. The speculoos crunch can be kept in an airtight container until ready to use.

16. For the whipped cream, combine the cream and icing sugar in a bowl and whisk to medium peaks. Set aside in the fridge until ready to assemble.

17. To assemble, place a spoonful of cherry compote in the bottom of the sundae glass. Fill the glass with 2 scoops of ice cream. Pour the warm hot fudge sauce over the ice cream. Place a heaping spoonful of cherry compote on top. Sprinkle on some candied almonds, then add a big dollop of whipped cream. Finish with a couple of spoonfuls of speculoos crunch and top with one more spoonful of cherry compote.

Chocolate Mocha Mud Pie

Makes one 8-inch round cake
Prep Time: 1 hour, 35 minutes
Cook Time: 20 minutes

½ cup (55 g) sliced almonds

Chocolate Crust
⅓ cup (75 g) unsalted butter

4½ cups (450 g) chocolate cookie crumbs

2 tablespoons (25 g) granulated sugar

1 quart coffee ice cream

Chocolate Sauce (page 238)

1 quart (1 L) Creamy Double Chocolate Ice Cream (page 169, or store-bought)

When I was a kid, my favorite birthday cake was an ice-cream cake with cookie crust. Sometimes my family would kick it up a notch with a decadent mocha mud pie from a local restaurant. I've created my own version of this delicious treat that I think stacks up, and today my kids carry on the tradition.

1. Preheat the oven to 325°F. Line the bottom of an 8-inch springform pan with parchment paper, then grease the entire inside of the pan or spray with nonstick spray.

2. Toast the almonds in the preheated oven for 10 minutes. Remove and set aside.

3. To make the chocolate crust, melt the butter in the microwave in 30-second increments. In a large bowl, combine the melted butter with the cookie crumbs and sugar. Mix well, then transfer to the springform pan. Evenly distribute the filling across the bottom and up the sides, right to the top of the rim. Using a glass with a flat bottom, compress the bottom of the crust and press it against the sides.

4. Bake the crust for 8 minutes. Remove from the oven and let cool completely.

5. Let the ice cream sit at room temperature for about 10 minutes.

6. Once the crust has cooled, spread the coffee ice cream over the bottom. Then spread a thin layer of chocolate sauce overtop. Place in the freezer for 10 minutes to set.

7. Spread the chocolate ice cream on top, making it as flat as possible; it should be almost level with the top of the pan. Apply another layer of chocolate sauce, and then sprinkle with the toasted almonds.

8. Return the mud pie to the freezer to set for 1 hour before enjoying.

Ice-Cream Truffle Pops

Makes 15 to 20 pops
Prep Time: 10 minutes, plus
1 hour for chilling

---

1 pint (500 ml) ice cream of
    your choice
11 oz (300 g) dark, milk or white
    couverture chocolate
Lollipop sticks

Suggested Toppings
Sprinkles
Candies
Crushed nuts
Crushed cookies

These are great little treats to have in your freezer for a quick sweet fix. This recipe is also a fun project to tackle with the kids on a weekend. The hardest part is picking your ice-cream flavor and toppings!

1. Using a #40 purple (¾ oz) ice-cream scoop, portion out ice-cream balls and place them on a baking sheet lined with parchment paper. Insert lollipop sticks into the tops, right into the middle of each ball, so they are all sticking straight up.

2. Place the baking sheet in the freezer until the pops are fully set and frozen, about 30 minutes.

3. Place your desired toppings in bowls.

4. Melt the chocolate in the microwave to 113°F (see page 7). Pour it into a narrow container with enough room to dip and fully coat the pops.

5. Pull the ice-cream pops out of the freezer and dip each one in the chocolate. If adding a coating, first dip the pop and then immediately roll it in the coating, before the chocolate sets. Then place it back on the baking sheet with the stick pointing up.

6. Place the dipped truffle pops in the freezer until fully set. To store, place them on their sides in an airtight container in the freezer.

Thirsty for Chocolate

Chocolate Peanut Butter Malt

Makes 1 glass
Prep Time: 5 minutes

---

3 scoops Creamy Double
   Chocolate Ice Cream
   (page 169, or store-bought)

½ cup (125 ml) whole milk

2 tablespoons (14 g) malted milk
   powder

1 tablespoon (15 g) smooth
   peanut butter

A malt is a lot like a milkshake. Both blend ice cream and milk, but a malt includes malted milk powder, which makes the drink creamier, richer and more flavorful. The malt adds a bitter roasted flavor that takes on the characteristics of chocolate. In this recipe I've added my favorite ingredient, peanut butter, which intensifies the nutty, bitter and sweet flavors.

1. Place the ice cream, milk, malted milk powder and peanut butter in a blender. Blend until well combined.

2. Pour into a glass and serve with a spoon.

NOTE
You can also use chocolate malted milk powder.

Iced Mocha Tiramisu Latte

Makes 1 glass
Prep Time: 5 minutes

---

2 oz (60 g) espresso or 1 cup
   (250 ml) brewed coffee

12 oz (360 g) ice, crushed

½ cup (125 ml) whole milk

1 tablespoon (15 ml) Baileys Irish
   Cream

2 tablespoons (30 ml) Mocha Syrup
   (page 238)

Whipped cream and chocolate
   shavings, for garnish

I love coffee, which is probably why I like tiramisu so much. If you do too, this is the ultimate summer drink for you—so easy to make and so refreshing. This latte is guaranteed to put a spring in your step on a hot summer afternoon.

1. Make the espresso or brew the coffee and set aside.

2. Fill a glass with the ice and pour in the milk and Baileys.

3. Add the mocha syrup to the espresso or coffee. Mix well.

4. Pour the coffee mixture over the milk and stir. Garnish with a little whipped cream and chocolate shavings.

See photos, page 198

The Ultimate
Chocolate Milkshake

Makes 1 glass
Prep Time: 5 minutes

¼ cup (60 ml) heavy cream

3 scoops vanilla ice cream

½ cup (125 ml) Chocolate Milk
(page 223) or regular whole milk

2 tablespoons (30 ml) Chocolate
Sauce (page 238), divided

Whipped cream, for garnish

Dark chocolate shavings,
(see page 13) for garnish

I remember going out for dinner with my parents to the local burger place and I couldn't wait to order a thick chocolate milkshake. Burger, fries and a shake—what else do you need? I know it sounds weird, but did you dip your fries into the shake too? Both salty and sweet, it's simply the best combination. Here I'm giving you the milkshake recipe and leaving it to you to decide whether you want fries with that.

1. Whisk the cream to medium peaks, then set aside.

2. Combine the ice cream, chocolate milk and 1 tablespoon of chocolate sauce in a blender. Blend well.

3. Pour into a milkshake glass. Garnish with a dollop of whipped cream. Drizzle the remaining 1 tablespoon chocolate sauce overtop, followed by chocolate shavings.

Chocolate Cream Soda

Makes 1 glass
Prep Time: 5 minutes

¼ cup (60 ml) whole milk

3 tablespoons (45 ml) Chocolate
Sauce (page 238)

1 cup (250 ml) carbonated water

2 scoops Creamy Double
Chocolate Ice Cream
(page 169, or store-bought)

Dark chocolate shavings
(see page 13), for garnish

Let's bring back some classics. Nothing recalls memories for me more than this drink. I remember being a kid in the summertime, raiding my mom's freezer on a hot day with my friends. A little vanilla ice cream (okay, lots of ice cream) in a cup, topped up with milk and soda water. Delicious!

1. Add the milk and chocolate syrup to a glass. Stir to fully combine.

2. Add the carbonated water and stir. Add the chocolate ice cream, garnish with chocolate shavings, and serve.

NOTE
You can also add whipped cream as a garnish if desired.

See photos, page 199

Chocolate Peanut Butter Malt

Iced Mocha Tiramisu Latte

The Ultimate Chocolate Milkshake

Chocolate Cream Soda

Chocolate Cherry Pisco Sour

Makes 1 cocktail
Prep Time: 10 minutes

Cherry Syrup

¼ cup (60 ml) water

¼ cup (45 g) pitted sour cherries, chopped

¼ cup (60 ml) cherry purée

Cocktail

1½ fl oz pisco

1 fl oz lemon juice

¼ fl oz cherry syrup

4 drops chocolate bitters, plus extra for garnish

1 egg white

Wine and chocolate make a classic pairing, but I've come to appreciate the incredible pairings available for chocolate in the world of spirits. Pisco is a clear distilled brandy liquor made from the bitter pisco grape. The Pisco Sour cocktail is traditionally made with lime juice, but I've made this one with lemon juice. I've also added cherry syrup to build a layer of sweetness into the taste profile.

1. For the cherry syrup, combine the water, chopped cherries and cherry purée in a pot and bring to a boil over medium-high heat. Boil for 2 minutes to infuse the flavors, then set aside to cool.

2. For the cocktail, fill a cocktail shaker with ice. Add the pisco, lemon juice, cherry syrup, chocolate bitters and egg white. Shake very well, until chilled.

3. Strain into a cocktail glass and garnish with 3 drops of chocolate bitters.

NOTE

You can substitute the sour cherries with sweet cherries, which will make the drink less sour.

If you do not have whole cherries, you can use more cherry purée.

For specialty syrups and purées, check online or try local gourmet food stores.

Chocolate Bramble

Makes 1 cocktail
Prep Time: 5 minutes

---

4 drops chocolate bitters

2 mint leaves, plus extra for garnish

4 blackberries, divided

Crushed ice

2 fl oz gin

1 fl oz lemon juice

4 teaspoons (20 ml) simple syrup

½ fl oz crème de cacao

Lemon peel, for garnish

It's just not summer until I've made something with blackberries. This noble berry stands up so well to any type of chocolate. I was introduced to the classic Bramble early in my culinary career. The British bartender behind this creation named it after the blackberry bush, which is also called a bramble. I've added chocolate because I find its bitterness perfectly balances the acidity of the lemon and blackberries.

1. Place the chocolate bitters, mint leaves and 2 blackberries in an old-fashioned glass and muddle them together. Then fill the glass with crushed ice.

2. Place the gin, lemon juice and simple syrup in a cocktail shaker filled with ice. Shake well.

3. Strain the cocktail into the glass, then pour in the crème de cacao.

4. Garnish with the remaining 2 blackberries, some mint leaves and a strip of the lemon peel.

Orange Chocolate Old-Fashioned

Makes 1 cocktail
Prep Time: 5 minutes

1 sugar cube
3 drops chocolate bitters
1 drop orange bitters
½ teaspoon soda water
½ fl oz crème de cacao
2 fl oz bourbon
Orange peel, for garnish

This classic cocktail should be a staple in everyone's repertoire. The Old-Fashioned is made with bourbon and orange bitters, both of which taste great with chocolate—so I've added a few chocolate twists to give this classic a new dimension of flavor.

1. Place the sugar cube, chocolate bitters and orange bitters in a cocktail glass and muddle them together. Then add the soda water.

2. Add 1 large ice cube to the glass. Add the crème de cacao and bourbon and give it a stir.

3. Garnish with a strip of orange peel.

NOTE

It's traditional to muddle the sugar with the bitters in the glass. However, you can substitute simple syrup for the sugar cube, or muddle in 1 cherry instead.

Brandy Alexander

Makes 1 cocktail
Prep Time: 3 minutes

1½ fl oz cognac
1 fl oz crème de cacao
½ fl oz half-and-half (10%) cream
Grated dark chocolate
(see page 13), for garnish

This traditionally gin-based cocktail hails from Britain, but somewhere along the way the recipe incorporated French cognac. Cognac is made from grapes, and I love how it plays in the glass with the chocolate-based crème de cacao. The bitter flavor and the cocoa fat of chocolate pair so well with the floral, spicy notes of the cognac.

1. Fill a cocktail shaker with ice. Add the cognac, crème de cacao and cream. Shake well, until chilled.

2. Strain into a chilled cocktail glass and garnish with grated chocolate.

See photos, page 206

Chocolate Clover Club

Makes 1 cocktail
Prep Time: 5 minutes

6 raspberries, divided
½ fl oz simple syrup
2 fl oz gin
½ fl oz white crème de cacao
½ fl oz lemon juice
1 egg white

The first time I sampled a Clover Club was at the famous Clover Club cocktail bar in Brooklyn. I was struck first by the fantastic forward flavor of raspberry, my favorite of all the berries. I like to find a prominent place for raspberries in everything I make, from breakfasts to desserts to my chocolate bonbons and cocktails. Adding white crème de cacao to this classic, in my humble opinion, creates an even richer delight to be savored.

1. Place 4 raspberries and the simple syrup in a cocktail shaker and muddle them together.

2. Add the gin, white crème de cacao, lemon juice and egg white to the shaker, along with some ice. Shake well, until fully chilled.

3. Strain into a chilled cocktail glass and garnish with the remaining 2 raspberries.

Chocolate Sidecar

Makes 1 cocktail
Prep Time: 5 minutes

2 fl oz cognac
1 fl oz crème de cacao
¾ fl oz lemon juice
½ fl oz triple sec
1 drop chocolate bitters
Orange peel, for garnish
Grated chocolate (see page 13),
   for garnish

Since I started getting into mixed drinks, I've become fascinated with classic cocktails and, in particular, the stories about how they were created. This one, for example, was invented in the 1920s in France and was named after the very popular motorcycle attachment of the day. Because of its prominent orange profile, it was ripe for a chocolate update.

1. Fill a cocktail shaker with ice. Add the cognac, crème de cacao, lemon juice, triple sec and chocolate bitters. Shake well, until chilled.

2. Strain into a cocktail glass and garnish with a strip of orange peel and grated chocolate.

See photos, page 207

Orange Chocolate Old-Fashioned

Brandy Alexander

Chocolate Clover Club

Chocolate Sidecar

Liquid Chocolate Bourbon Ball

Makes 1 cocktail

Prep Time: 5 minutes

1½ fl oz bourbon

½ fl oz crème de cacao

½ fl oz hazelnut liqueur

1 egg white

4 drops chocolate bitters

Dark chocolate shavings
(see page 13), for garnish

Wafer crumbs, for garnish

The bourbon ball has been a Southern delicacy since the 1930s. It's a truffle-like dessert from Kentucky made with bourbon, pecans, wafer crumbs and chocolate. It seemed to me like the perfect concoction to turn into a cocktail. The sweet bourbon and bitter chocolate taste like bluegrass in a glass.

1. Fill a cocktail shaker halfway with ice.

2. Add the bourbon, crème de cacao, hazelnut liqueur and egg white to the shaker.

3. Shake well, until chilled, and strain into a cocktail glass. Add the chocolate bitters.

4. Garnish with dark chocolate shavings and wafer crumbs.

Orange and Lime Chocolate Margarita

Makes 1 cocktail
Prep Time: 5 minutes

Rim Garnish
1.6 oz (40 g) dark chocolate
1 teaspoon fleur de sel
Splash of fresh orange juice
Fresh lime wedges

Lime Simple Syrup
1 cup (200 g) granulated sugar
1 cup (250 ml) fresh lime juice

Cocktail
1 fl oz tequila
½ fl oz crème de cacao
½ fl oz fresh orange juice
½ fl oz lime simple syrup

My wife, Lara, makes the best margaritas. It's our go-to cocktail at home on the weekend. A margarita hits every flavor note—it's refreshing, sweet, sour and salty. Which, of course, makes it a perfect canvas for chocolate. So Lara and I decided to mix up our classic recipe by adding a little chocolate. We think it's a keeper.

1. For the rim garnish, grate the chocolate and lightly mix it with the fleur de sel. Do not overmix or the heat from your hands will melt the chocolate. Rub the rim of the glass with orange juice to moisten it, then dip it into the mixture to coat.

2. To make the lime syrup, combine the sugar and lime juice in a pot and bring to a boil. Set aside and let cool. (You will only use a little of the syrup. You can store the rest in an airtight container in the fridge for up to 2 weeks.)

3. Fill a cocktail shaker with ice. Add the tequila, crème de cacao, orange juice and lime simple syrup. Shake well, until chilled.

4. Strain into the garnished glass, add a lime wedge and enjoy.

Paper Plane
with a Chocolate Twist

Makes 1 cocktail
Prep Time: 5 minutes

1 fl oz bourbon
1 fl oz Aperol
1 fl oz Amaro Nonino
1 fl oz lemon juice
5 drops chocolate bitters

I recently tried a Paper Plane cocktail for the first time at a restaurant in Toronto. I had never heard of it, so the pastry chef, who was also a bartender, whipped it up for me, and it quickly became my new favorite. It's refreshing, sweet and a little bitter. I decided to add chocolate and I just couldn't believe it tasted even better!

1. In a cocktail shaker filled with ice, combine the bourbon, Aperol, Amaro Nonino, lemon juice and chocolate bitters. Shake well, until chilled.

2. Strain into a cocktail glass and enjoy.

Shaken Chocolate Martini

Makes 1 cocktail
Prep Time: 5 minutes

Cocoa powder, for garnish
2 fl oz Nikka Coffey vodka
½ fl oz Martini dry (white) vermouth
¼ fl oz white crème de cacao,
   plus extra to rim the glass
Dark couverture chocolate curl
   (see page 13), for garnish

When I think of martinis, I think of them in a classy setting like a dinner party or a great cocktail bar. I'm a big fan of vodka martinis and I love to experiment with different brands of vodka. I've traveled the world eating and drinking with one of my best friends, Brett, who is a master chocolatier, and we're always swapping details about food and cocktails. The amazing vodka he recommended for this cocktail comes from Japan. It pairs so well with chocolate that I encourage you to get your hands on it, but if you can't, another premium vodka will work well too.

1. Rim the edge of a martini glass with some crème de cacao, then dip it into the cocoa powder to coat.

2. In a cocktail shaker filled with ice, combine the vodka, vermouth and crème de cacao. Shake well, until chilled.

3. Strain into the rimmed glass and garnish with a chocolate curl.

Paper Plane with a Chocolate Twist

Shaken Chocolate Martini

White Chocolate Negroni

Makes 1 cocktail

Prep Time: 3 minutes

½ fl oz dry gin

½ fl oz Campari

½ fl oz sweet vermouth

½ fl oz white crème de cacao

3 drops chocolate bitters,
   for garnish

White chocolate curls, for garnish

Fresh orange slices, for garnish

I love the classic Negroni cocktail. It's got just three ingredients in equal parts. Making room for a fourth (chocolate) ingredient is worth it. The sweetness of the crème de cacao balances this cocktail's bitterness.

1. In a glass filled with ice, combine the gin, Campari, vermouth and crème de cacao. Using a spoon or stir stick, stir for 20 seconds.

2. Strain into a fresh glass over 1 large ice cube. Garnish with the chocolate bitters, white chocolate curls and orange slices.

Kid-Friendly Chocolate

Easy-Made Chocolate Bars

Makes five 2.3-ounce (65 g) bars
Prep Time: 15 minutes

11 oz (325 g) dark, milk, ruby
or white chocolate

Filling/Topping Ideas

Freeze-dried fruits

Shredded coconut

Crushed nuts

Gummy bears

Sprinkles

Spices

Flaky salt

Cereal

Candies

Making chocolate bars is easy and fun to do, especially at home with the kids. All you need is tempered chocolate, a mold and your favorite flavorings. Just add the filling(s), pour the chocolate into the molds and sprinkle on your toppings. You can also fold flavor into the chocolate itself, with something like toffee bits. I guarantee you'll eat these bars in a second!

1. Start by tempering the chocolate, following the instructions on page 8.

2. Once the chocolate is tempered, add any filling you like (some ideas are listed here).

3. Pour the chocolate into the bar mold of your choice. Tap the mold on the counter to remove any air bubbles. Using a bench scraper or offset spatula, scrape across the mold to smooth out the chocolate and make it level with the top.

4. Add your choice of toppings and leave to set.

NOTE

Store the chocolate bars in an airtight container in a cool, dry, dark place. If stored properly, the shelf life of the bars is up to 1 year. You can use a variety of ingredients to top the chocolate bar for color, texture and flavor. Choose whatever you like best!

Milk Chocolate–Covered Caramel Apples

Makes 8 apples
Prep Time: 10 minutes
Cook Time: 20 minutes

8 Granny Smith apples
1¾ cups (425 ml) heavy cream
1¼ cups (250 g) light brown sugar
¾ cup (245 g) corn syrup
¾ cup (175 g) unsalted butter
28 oz (800 g) milk chocolate, tempered

Suggested Toppings

Crushed cookies
Mini candies
Chopped nuts
Sparkles
Mini marshmallows
Crushed pretzels
Toasted coconut

Your kids will go crazy over these caramel apples. I like to use a firmer apple, for added crunch. Granny Smith apples are great because they have a tartness that complements the sweetness of the caramel and chocolate. Have fun, get creative with the kids, and let their imagination take over.

1. Wash and dry the apples. Insert 7-inch wooden skewers into the tops, through the middle of the core. Place in the fridge to get cold.

2. Line a baking sheet with parchment paper and set aside.

3. To make the caramel, combine the cream, brown sugar, corn syrup and butter in a pot. Place over medium heat. Cook, stirring, until the temperature reaches 240°F on a candy thermometer, about 10 to 12 minutes. Stirring will prevent it from burning on the bottom of the pot.

4. Remove the pot from the heat and strain the caramel into a bowl that's deep enough to fully submerge the apples. Allow the caramel to cool for 10 minutes.

5. Remove the apples from the fridge. One at a time, dip an apple into the caramel until fully submerged. Pull it out by twisting the stick to help the excess caramel drip off. Allow the caramel to set for 20 seconds, then dip one more time, again swirling to remove excess caramel. Place on the parchment-lined baking sheet to set. Repeat this process with all the apples.

6. Set the apples aside for 20 minutes to allow them to cool fully.

7. Place the tempered chocolate in a bowl that's deep enough to fully submerge the apples.

8. Dip each apple once into the chocolate, using the same swirling motion as before to remove excess chocolate.

9. If you are adding a topping, do so immediately after the apple comes out of the chocolate. You have to move quickly or the chocolate will set. You can spread your desired topping out in a shallow bowl and roll the apple overtop, or use your hands to pat the topping on. Have fun with it!

10. Once the apples are topped, return them to the baking sheet to set before enjoying.

Chocolate Lollipops

Makes 10–12 lollipops
Prep Time: 5 minutes,
plus 10 minutes for setting

---

12 oz (340 g) dark, milk, ruby
or white chocolate
Plastic or silicone molds
Lollipop sticks

These lollipops are just fun to have in the house. They're the perfect treat to serve at birthday parties or for the kids to take to class for Halloween, Easter or Valentine's Day. Once you learn how to temper chocolate, you can turn it into your favorite shapes or characters. Head to your local craft store and see what's in stock for lollipop molds. You can find the sticks there too.

1. Start by tempering the chocolate (see page 8).

2. Transfer the tempered chocolate to a piping bag. Cut a small piece off the tip of the piping bag and pipe the chocolate into the molds.

3. Gently bang the molds on your work surface to even out the chocolate and remove any air bubbles. Place the lollipop sticks in the middle of the chocolate, giving them a slight roll to coat.

4. Place the lollipops in the fridge for 10 minutes to set, then unmold.

NOTE
You can enjoy these lollipops as they are, or you can dip them into hot milk for a decadent hot chocolate.

Chocolate Milk

Makes 1 serving
Prep Time: 3 minutes

1¾ cups (425 ml) milk
3 tablespoons (45 ml) Chocolate
Sauce (page 238)

I used to love wearing down my mom in the dairy section of the grocery store. "Mom, can I get some chocolate milk? Can I? Can I?" She always said yes, but to this day it still feels like a special treat. I love substituting chocolate milk for regular milk in recipes, to add a little something special. It's easy to make yourself, so you'll never run out.

1. Combine the milk and chocolate sauce in a large cup and whisk together to combine fully.

2. Store in the fridge and drink cold.

Hot Chocolate 3 Ways

Makes one 8-ounce mug
Prep Time: 2 minutes
Cook Time: 2 minutes

Salted Dark Hot Chocolate

¼ cup (60 ml) heavy cream, for garnish

1 cup (250 ml) whole milk

1.5 oz (45 g) dark chocolate pailletés

1 teaspoon Dutch-process cocoa powder

⅛ teaspoon flaky salt

Milk Chocolate Caramel Hot Chocolate

¼ cup (60 ml) heavy cream, for garnish

1 cup (250 ml) whole milk

1.5 oz (45 g) milk chocolate pailletés

2 tablespoons (30 ml) Dark Chocolate Caramel Sauce (page 234)

White Chocolate Matcha Hot Chocolate

¼ cup (60 ml) heavy cream, for garnish

1 cup (250 ml) whole milk

3 oz (80 g) white chocolate pailletés

1 tablespoon (12 g) matcha powder

Hot chocolate was (and still is) a staple in our house. It tastes even better once the weather turns cool, especially after a day of skiing. It's one of the easiest drinks to make, and one of the best things to enjoy with family. I've amped up this hot chocolate with different flavors, but in the end, you can never go wrong with the classic.

1. Whichever version you're making, whip the cream for the garnish.

2. Combine the milk and the chocolate pailletés in a pot and set it over low heat. Whisk together constantly until the chocolate has melted, creating a frothy consistency.

3. Remove from the heat and whisk in the flavoring.

4. Pour into a mug and spoon the whipped cream on top.

NOTE

For any of these drinks, garnish with chocolate shavings, grated chocolate, caramel sauce or matcha powder, if desired.

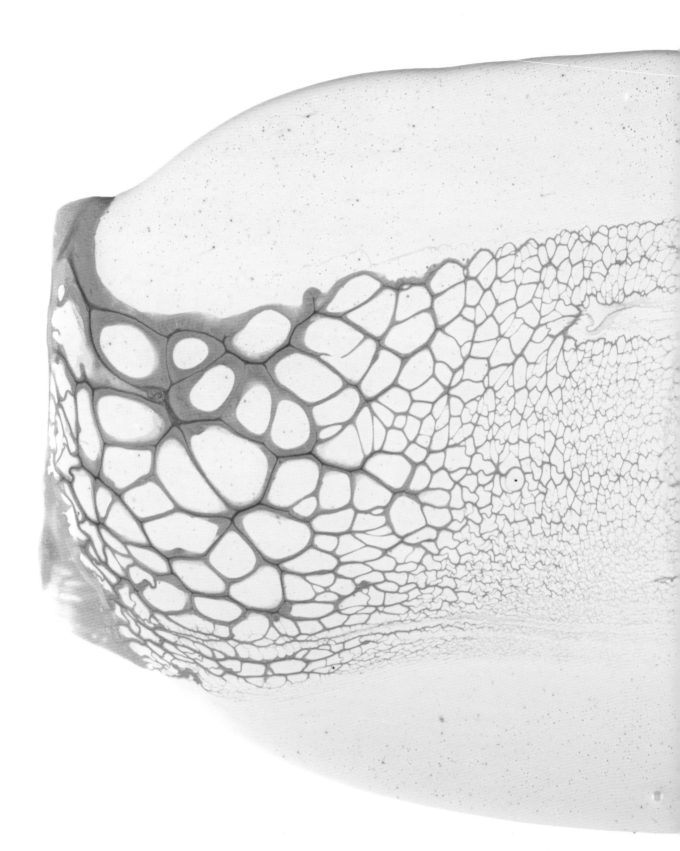

Essential Fillings & Desserts

Chocolate Crème Brûlée

Makes six 5-ounce servings

Prep Time: 40 minutes, plus 2 hours to set

Cook Time: 25 to 30 minutes

---

8 egg yolks

1 cup (200 g) granulated sugar

3 cups + 2 tablespoons (780 ml) heavy cream

1 vanilla bean

3.5 oz (100 g) 70% chocolate, roughly chopped

⅓ cup (70 g) fine sugar

Crème brûlée is probably one of the best-known desserts in the world, and when it's done right, it appears simple but is actually full of rich, decadent flavors. Although it's most often served as a vanilla custard, crème brûlée is also a great opportunity to play with chocolate flavors. That caramelized sugar crunch layer is my favorite part!

1. Preheat the oven to 300°F.

2. Place the egg yolks and granulated sugar in a bowl and whisk together to fully combine.

3. Place the cream and vanilla bean in a pot and bring to a simmer over medium heat.

4. Remove the pot from the heat. Add half of the cream to the egg mixture, whisking vigorously. Then add the mixture to the pot with the remaining cream. Whisk again to fully combine.

5. Place the chopped chocolate in a large bowl. Strain the cream mixture over the bowl, whisking to melt the chocolate.

6. Divide the custard mixture evenly among 6 ramekins. Carefully place the ramekins in a deep baking or roasting pan. Create a water bath by adding water to the pan halfway up the sides of the ramekins. Don't splash any water into the ramekins!

7. Cover the baking dish with foil and carefully transfer to the preheated oven. Bake for 40 minutes, then check the custards to see if they are set. If the mixture is still wobbly in the middle, bake them for another 5 minutes, then check again. Repeat the process until they are set.

8. Remove the ramekins from the water bath, place on a cold baking sheet, and refrigerate for about 2 hours to set firmly.

9. Just before you're ready to serve, sprinkle about 2 teaspoons of fine sugar evenly over each custard. Using a kitchen torch, caramelize the sugar to a light golden color. Serve immediately.

NOTE

The custards can be stored in the fridge for up to 5 days.

Chocolate Pastry Cream

Makes 2½ cups
Prep Time: 10 minutes
Cook Time: 10 minutes

---

1 cup (250 ml) whole milk

3 large egg yolks

¼ cup (50 g) granulated sugar

3 tablespoons (22 g) cornstarch

2 tablespoons (30 g) unsalted butter, room temperature

2.2 oz (60 g) dark chocolate

Versatile pastry cream is one of my favorite custard bases. It can be used as a filling for cakes, tarts and pastries; it's great in parfait cups or trifles; and it's delicious on its own with some fresh fruit. You can use milk or white chocolate instead of dark, or leave out the chocolate altogether and let the vanilla flavor shine through. This is a simple recipe, but a great one to master.

1. Place the milk in a medium pot and bring to a boil over medium-high heat. Set aside.

2. In a bowl, whisk together the egg yolks, sugar and cornstarch.

3. Pour half the hot milk into the egg mixture, whisking to fully combine. Then add the mixture to the remaining milk, whisking continuously.

4. Return the pot to the stovetop over medium-low heat and bring the mixture to a boil, whisking constantly so it doesn't burn or overcook. Once it starts to bubble, immediately remove from the heat and transfer the mixture to the bowl of a stand mixer fitted with the whisk attachment. Whisk at medium speed to fully cool it down.

5. Once the mixture is cool, keep the mixer running and slowly add the butter, a little bit at a time. Keep whisking to emulsify the pastry cream.

6. Melt the chocolate in a heatproof bowl in the microwave in 10-second increments (see page 7). Slowly add the melted chocolate to the pastry cream, whisking to incorporate fully.

7. Transfer the pastry cream to an airtight container and store in the fridge.

NOTE

The pastry cream will last for up to 1 week in the fridge. I don't recommend freezing it, as it can separate.

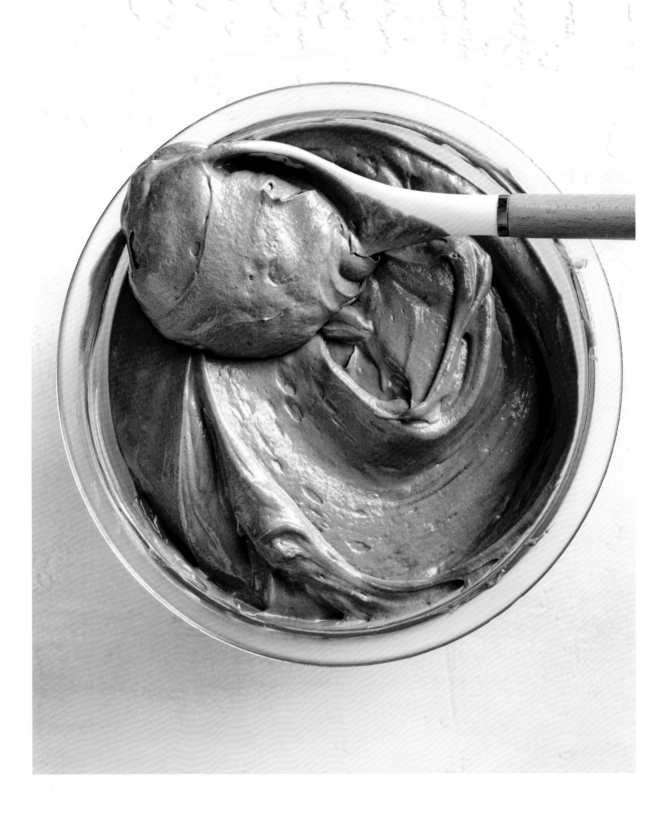

Chocolate Italian Buttercream

Makes 3 cups
Prep Time: 15 minutes
Cook Time: 3 minutes

---

3 large egg whites

1 cup (200 g) granulated sugar

3 tablespoons (45 ml) water

1⅓ cups (300 g) unsalted butter, room temperature

3 oz (75 g) melted dark chocolate

I prefer Italian buttercream over American buttercream. The Italian version is creamier, less sweet and richer in flavor because it contains equal quantities of butter and sugar, while American buttercream uses much more sugar than butter. This classic recipe calls for the sugar to be cooked, which makes for a more stable cream—perfect to use between cake layers, and great in tarts or as a filling for sandwich cookies. In Steve's Sandwich Cookies (page 163), you can replace the cream cheese frosting with this buttercream for equal deliciousness.

1. Place the egg whites in the bowl of a stand mixer fitted with the whisk attachment. Mix on low speed until the whites start to look frothy.

2. Combine the sugar and water in a pot and cook over high heat until the temperature reaches 245°F. Remove from the heat and allow the bubbles to subside.

3. Increase the speed of the mixer and whisk the egg whites to full volume.

4. Reduce the speed to low and slowly pour in the hot sugar syrup, down the side of the bowl. Increase the speed to high and whisk until the mixture is fully cooled and comes to full volume.

5. Keep mixing and slowly add the butter, a bit at a time. Mix until the mixture is fully emulsified and starts looking like buttercream.

6. Mix in the melted chocolate. Scrape down the bottom and sides of the bowl to make sure that it's fully incorporated.

7. Place the buttercream in the fridge or freezer, depending on when you need to use it. Before using, bring it to room temperature. Then place in the bowl of a stand mixer fitted with the paddle attachment and whip to bring it back to full volume.

NOTE

The buttercream can be frozen for up to 6 months.

Dark Chocolate Caramel Sauce

Makes 2½ cups

Prep Time: 5 minutes, plus 1 hour cooling

Cook Time: 10 minutes

1⅓ cups + 5 teaspoons (350 ml) heavy cream

2½ tablespoons (50 g) corn syrup

1 cup (200 g) granulated sugar

1.8 oz (50 g) dark chocolate, chopped

¾ cup (175 g) unsalted butter, room temperature

If you don't already have caramel sauce on hand in your house, you're missing out. Caramel is one of those things that makes everything taste better, whether it's cake or ice cream. Melting sugar and caramelizing it changes the flavor, and once it turns golden brown, it develops a nuttiness that is absolutely delicious. Adding dark chocolate helps to soften the sweetness from the sugar content.

1. Combine the cream and corn syrup in a pot and bring to a boil. Set aside.

2. In a separate pot, make a dry caramel with the sugar. Add one-third of the sugar and melt over low heat. Once it's melted, repeat twice more, always waiting until the sugar has melted before adding the next batch. Once it is fully dissolved, keep stirring to create that light golden color, making sure no sugar granules remain.

3. Slowly add the warm cream mixture to the sugar, whisking continuously to make sure it does not boil over.

4. Once fully combined, boil the caramel for 2 minutes. Remove from the heat and stir in the chocolate. Allow the mixture to cool completely at room temperature, about 1 hour. Once cooled, add the butter. Use an immersion blender to emulsify the mixture and enjoy.

NOTE

Cooling the caramel before emulsifying the sauce will prevent the butter from splitting.

Hot Fudge Sauce

Makes 2 cups
Prep Time: 5 minutes
Cook Time: 15 minutes

½ cup (125 ml) water

½ cup (100 g) granulated sugar

⅓ cup (75 ml) heavy cream

⅛ cup + 1 teaspoon (45 g)
corn syrup

5 oz (150 g) dark chocolate,
chopped

When I was growing up, I couldn't wait for the weekend and family movie night. Pizza and hot fudge sundaes were always on the menu—vanilla ice cream, crushed nuts and tons of hot fudge sauce. It's still the best way to wrap up a week, and something that my kids look forward to these days.

1. Combine the water, sugar, cream and corn syrup in a pot and bring to a boil.

2. Place the chocolate in a bowl. Once the sugar mixture has boiled, pour it into the bowl and stir to melt the chocolate.

3. Strain the sauce into a container. Allow it to cool, then store in the fridge in an airtight container.

4. When ready to use, warm the sauce in the microwave in 30-second increments, then pour over your favorite ice cream. The fudge sauce can be frozen for up to 6 months.

Chocolate Sauce

Makes 2 cups
Prep Time: 10 minutes
Cook Time: 5 minutes

---

²/₃ cup (150 g) granulated sugar

½ cup (125 ml) water

6 tablespoons (50 g) Dutch-process cocoa powder

¾ cup (175 ml) heavy cream

1 oz (25 g) dark chocolate, chopped

This sauce should always be in your fridge, because you never know when you'll want to add some to your coffee in the morning, your milkshake in the afternoon or a cocktail in the evening. This is slightly thick and has a beautiful shine and an intense chocolate flavor.

1. Combine the sugar and water in a pot. Bring the mixture to a boil.

2. Sift in the cocoa powder and emulsify, using a whisk, until fully combined.

3. Add the cream and bring back to a boil for 1 minute.

4. Place the chopped chocolate in a bowl. Strain the cream mixture into the bowl. Using a whisk or immersion blender, emulsify the sauce.

5. The sauce can be stored in the fridge for up to 2 weeks or in the freezer for up to 6 months.

NOTE

If you store this sauce in the freezer, remove it the night before using and put it in the fridge to thaw.

Mocha Syrup

Makes 2 cups
Prep Time: 10 minutes
Cook Time: 3 minutes

1½ cups (375 ml) brewed espresso

1 cup (200 g) granulated sugar

¼ cup (30 g) Dutch-process cocoa powder

3 oz (80 g) dark chocolate, chopped

1 teaspoon vanilla extract

If you're both a coffee drinker and a chocolate lover like me (I may overdo it a bit—no, actually, you never can), make room for this syrup in the fridge. It adds a punch of caffeine and a hint of sweetness to your coffee, and it's also a great topping for ice cream and desserts.

1. In a pot, combine the espresso, sugar and cocoa powder. Bring to a boil.

2. Remove from the heat and add the chopped chocolate. Stir until fully combined and the chocolate has melted. Then stir in the vanilla. Allow the syrup to cool completely.

3. Strain the syrup into an airtight container and store in the fridge for up to 1 week.

NOTE

Have fun by replacing the vanilla extract with other flavorings, such as almond extract.

Mocha Syrup

White Chocolate Crème Anglaise

Makes 2 cups
Prep Time: 5 minutes
Cook Time: 5 minutes

---

2 cups (500 ml) whole milk

4 large egg yolks

¼ cup (50 g) granulated sugar

3.5 oz (100 g) white chocolate, chopped

Sauces are a great addition to just about any dessert. They're a quick and easy way to boost the flavor and add another layer of richness to the plate. White chocolate crème anglaise is sweet, so it pairs well with desserts, soufflés and ice creams that are subtle in flavor, acidic or bitter. This sauce would be great on Flourless Chocolate Cake (page 57), Chocolate Lava Cakes (page 90) and even Chocolate Soufflés (page 80). But don't stop at using just white chocolate; try milk or dark chocolate instead.

1. In a medium pot, bring the milk to a boil over medium-high heat. Remove from the heat to cool slightly.

2. Prepare an ice bath and set it aside.

3. In a bowl, whisk together the egg yolks and sugar until light and airy.

4. Temper the egg mixture by pouring in half of the hot milk and whisking to fully combine. Then pour the mixture back into the pot with the remaining milk. Return to the stove over low heat and cook until it coats the back of a spoon. If you're using a thermometer, it should reach 180°F and will be thick.

5. Place the chocolate in a large bowl with a fine-mesh strainer set overtop. Strain the milk mixture over the chocolate. Emulsify with a whisk until the chocolate is fully melted.

6. Cool the bowl in the ice bath, then transfer the sauce to an airtight container. The crème anglaise will keep in the fridge for up to 5 days.

NOTE

You can infuse flavors into this crème anglaise using herbs, spices or oils such as mint, rosemary, lemongrass, tarragon, hot peppers, orange oil or peppermint extract. Boil the milk with the flavoring first and steep for 10 minutes, then strain and continue with Step 2.

Milk Chocolate Hazelnut Spread

Makes 2 cups
Prep Time: 15 minutes, plus 2 hours, 30 minutes for setting
Cook Time: 20 minutes

---

11 oz (315 g) chopped blanched hazelnuts, shells and skins removed

5.6 oz (160 g) milk couverture chocolate

¼ cup (30 g) Dutch-process cocoa powder

¼ cup (60 ml) vegetable oil

3 tablespoons (24 g) icing sugar

Hazelnuts are at the top of my list of nuts that pair well with chocolate. I know that if you're a chocolate lover you probably feel the same way, thanks to the many chocolate hazelnut spreads available in supermarkets. When roasted, the nuttiness of hazelnuts balances so well with the bitterness of the chocolate. I use milk chocolate in this recipe because it's creamy and sweet, which balances the earthiness of the hazelnuts.

1. Preheat the oven to 325°F and place the hazelnuts on a baking sheet. Toast in the oven for about 20 minutes, until golden brown. Let cool completely.

2. Place the hazelnuts in a food processor and blend until they break down and start to resemble a paste, scraping down the bowl and mixing the nuts together occasionally. This should take about 5 minutes in total.

3. Once the hazelnuts begin to look like a paste, add the chocolate, cocoa powder, vegetable oil and icing sugar. Blitz until ultra-smooth; this should take about 5 minutes, but remember to keep scraping down the bowl.

4. Transfer the spread to a jar and place in the fridge for about 2½ hours to set.

NOTE

You can change the type of chocolate you use to create different flavors.

If the mixture sets too hard to your liking, stir in a little more oil.

Chocolate hazelnut spread makes a great jarred gift.

Chocolate Mirror Glaze

Makes enough for a 9-inch round cake

Prep Time: 5 minutes

Cook Time: 10 minutes

---

9 gelatin sheets or 2¼ tablespoons (18 g) powdered gelatin

½ cup (125 ml) heavy cream

½ cup (150 g) corn syrup

½ cup (100 g) granulated sugar

3 tablespoons (45 ml) water

1 cup (120 g) Dutch-process cocoa powder

When it comes to taking your cakes to the next level, it's all about the details. Glazing a cake gives it shine and elevates its sophistication. This glaze is perfect for cakes that call for a chocolatey finishing touch.

1. Bloom the gelatin sheets in cold water until fully hydrated, about 5 minutes. Remove from the water and squeeze out any excess. If using powdered gelatin, the ratio is 5 parts water to 1 part powdered gelatin.

2. Combine the cream and corn syrup in a microwave-safe bowl and warm in the microwave for 45 seconds. It should be warm to the touch. Test with a finger, and add 5 more seconds if needed, then set aside.

3. Place the sugar and water in a pot and cook over medium heat until it reaches 255°F.

4. Immediately add the cream mixture to the sugar syrup and whisk until fully combined.

5. Remove the pot from the heat and, using a candy thermometer, let the mixture cool until it reaches 122°F. Add the gelatin and whisk until it is fully melted.

6. Strain into a container. Cool the mixture to 90°F before using.

NOTE

Glazes can be made in advance and stored in the fridge for up to 2 weeks or in the freezer for up to 6 months.

When ready to glaze a cake, warm the mirror glaze to 90°F. If it's too warm, it will run off, but at the right temperature it will adhere to the cake and hold its shine.

White Chocolate Mirror Glaze

Makes 6 cups
Prep Time: 10 minutes
Cook Time: 5 minutes

7½ gelatin sheets or 1½ tablespoons (15 g) powdered gelatin

1½ cups (300 g) granulated sugar

¾ cup + 1½ tablespoons (275 g) corn syrup

1⅓ cups + 2 tablespoons (360 ml) condensed milk

½ cup + ⅓ cup (205 ml) water

11.2 oz (320 g) white couverture chocolate, chopped

1 oz (28 ml) oil-based white food coloring

The great thing about white glazes is that you can have fun with color. You can keep half of it white and color the other half, then use a toothpick or cake tester to drag the colors together—or get inspired with a design of your own. This white chocolate version is shiny and sweet, with a great wow factor.

1. Bloom the gelatin sheets in cold water until fully hydrated, about 5 minutes. Remove from the water and squeeze out any excess. If using powdered gelatin, the ratio is 5 parts water to 1 part powdered gelatin.

2. In a pot, combine the sugar, corn syrup, condensed milk and water. Bring to a boil.

3. Remove the pot from the heat, add the bloomed gelatin and stir until fully dissolved.

4. Place the chopped chocolate in a bowl. Pour the hot mixture over the chocolate and emulsify until smooth, using a whisk or immersion blender. Add the food coloring and emulsify again.

5. Strain into a container. Cool the mixture to 90°F before using.

Milk Chocolate Pudding with Fresh Kiwis

Makes 4 servings

Prep Time: 15 minutes, plus 30 minutes for setting

Cook Time: 8 minutes

Pudding

¼ cup (50 g) granulated sugar

¼ cup (30 g) Dutch-process cocoa powder

1½ tablespoons (12 g) cornstarch

1 cup + 2 tablespoons (280 ml) whole milk

½ cup (125 ml) heavy cream

1 teaspoon vanilla extract

4 oz (115 g) milk couverture chocolate, chopped

2 large kiwis

Whipped Cream

¾ cup (175 ml) heavy cream

1 tablespoon (8 g) icing sugar

I love custard-based chocolate desserts, and chocolate pudding is one of the most versatile comfort foods around. Everyone embraces the idea of one like a warm hug. Puddings can stand alone or become a beautiful filling for desserts. They also taste great with fresh fruit or a compote. Here I'm using bright, tart kiwis. Milk chocolate balances their acidity while nudging out the sweetness of the fruit.

1. To make the pudding, place the sugar, cocoa powder and cornstarch in a medium pot, off the heat. Whisk together.

2. Whisk in the milk, cream and vanilla. Bring to a boil over medium heat, whisking continuously, until the mixture becomes thick. Remove from the heat and whisk in the chocolate until it has fully melted.

3. Transfer the mixture into 4 serving dishes and place in the fridge until set, about 30 minutes.

4. Dice the kiwis and set aside.

5. Before serving, make the whipped cream by whisking together the cream and icing sugar to medium peaks.

6. Spoon diced kiwi over top, then dollop with whipped cream.

White Chocolate and Orange Panna Cotta

Makes five 6-ounce servings
Prep Time: 5 minutes, plus 2 hours for setting
Cook Time: 5 minutes

Panna Cotta

4 gelatin sheets or 1 tablespoon (8 g) gelatin powder

2⅓ cups (560 ml) heavy cream

¾ cup + 2 tablespoons (205 ml) whole milk

1 medium orange, zested

1 vanilla bean, split and scraped

2 tablespoons (25 g) granulated sugar

1 tablespoon (15 ml) Grand Marnier

9.7 oz (275 g) white chocolate, chopped

Candied Orange Zest

1 large orange

½ cup (100 g) granulated sugar

½ cup (125 ml) water

Panna cotta is a luscious custard dessert, but because it uses gelatin rather than eggs, it's much lighter than a crème brûlée or crème caramel. When I was working in restaurants, it was an easy dessert to execute quickly. I didn't have to worry about overcooking it like a custard and it was always consistent. You can flavor panna cotta with all sorts of things, and it's always delicious served with fresh fruit or coulis.

1. For the panna cotta, bloom the gelatin sheets in cold water until fully hydrated, about 5 minutes. Remove from the water and squeeze out any excess. If using powdered gelatin, the ratio is 5 parts water to 1 part powdered gelatin.

2. In a medium pot, combine the cream, milk, orange zest, vanilla bean and seeds, and sugar. Bring to a boil over medium-high heat.

3. Prepare an ice bath and set it aside.

4. Once the cream mixture has boiled, remove it from the heat and add the bloomed gelatin and Grand Marnier. Stir until the gelatin has fully dissolved.

5. Place the white chocolate in a large bowl with a fine-mesh strainer set overtop. Strain the cream mixture over the chocolate. Whisk together until fully combined.

6. Place the bowl of panna cotta in the ice bath and cool. Strain into a separate clean bowl with a pouring spout, then pour into individual dishes to set. Refrigerate for at least 2 hours.

7. For the candied orange zest, carefully remove the peel from the orange, using a paring knife (make sure not to include the white pith). Slice the peel into long, thin strands.

8. Place the zest in a small pot and pour in water just to cover. Bring to a boil, then immediately strain off the water. Repeat this process 2 more times. Set aside the zest.

9. Next, make a simple syrup. In a pot, combine the sugar and water. Bring to a boil over medium-high heat, and boil until the sugar has dissolved completely. Remove the pot from the heat, transfer the syrup to a container and add the orange zest. Allow the zest to soak for 1 hour before using it. It will last for up to 1 month in the fridge, stored in the syrup.

10. Remove the panna cotta dishes from the fridge and garnish with candied orange zest.

Acknowledgments
& Index

Acknowledgments

Looking back, I think my culinary journey has been leading me to develop this book. Every failure and every success have been my teachers. And along the way I have had tremendous guidance and support from my family and friends.

To my wife, Lara (whom I affectionately call Bob Victoria Woo-Woo), you have been with me since the start of my career, helping me interpret the guideposts along the path. You have watched me grow as a chef and supported every move I made, without judgment and with complete support. You have generously made it possible for me to travel, work, explore new opportunities and find the space and time to write this book, all while lovingly raising our two children, Charlie and Levi. Thank you.

Charlie and Levi have been the best taste-testers throughout this process. Charlie, you are already famous with our clientele at Temper. You were born the year we opened the shop and you have a product named after you that's hands down the most popular item we sell, since day one—the "Charlie Bite." Charlie and Levi have liked everything on their fork, and I'm guessing that may be because there are so many desserts to be tested. I thank you from the bottom of my heart for your patience, understanding and support. I love you.

To my sisters, Ali, Kristen and Jamie, you have always supported me, even while putting up with my brotherly annoyances. To my middle sister, Kristen, my business partner in Temper Chocolate & Pastry, you have made it possible for me to take time away from the business to pursue other opportunities, without the worry of managing the day-to-day operations. You have steered the business to new heights, all while raising a beautiful family of your own. Thank you for your steady hand and unconditional support.

Ali, my oldest sister and constant cheerleader, you have always stood by my side. In fact, you were the original driving force keeping us on track when we opened the doors at Temper. We miss you—please come back to work.

And finally, thank you to my youngest sister, Jamie, the creative force behind Jamie Lauren photography. She provided photography and food styling for this book, and so much more. Jamie, you are the backbone of this cookbook. Your creative talents have brought everything together visually and far beyond my imagination. Your photography is one-of-a-kind; it has been rewarding to watch you bring your creative vision for this book to life. Thank you for being an important part of the journey.

Jimmy Jeong, of Jimmy Shoots, your photography speaks for itself. You have been taking photos for Temper throughout the years. You are calm and contemplative in your approach to the work. Your photos always tell a story, and I'm so pleased with the stories you conveyed through the photos in this book. Thank you, my man.

Carole and Brett Roy, thank you for your ongoing support and friendship. Carole, when the timing got tight and I didn't know where else to turn, you stepped up and helped me clarify my vision for this book. You helped guide me through each chapter, putting my thoughts into words. Brett, where do I start? From the day we met, you have been a friend, brother, mentor, chef and inspiration. Your knowledge and love for food always keep me excited and motivated to experiment. I consider you one of the best chefs I've ever known and I'm so proud to have you in my life. The many years of cooking and traveling with you have inspired so many of the recipes in this book. Our talks about food and life experiences are an important part of my day. There is no better person than you.

Dad, there is so much from you I am grateful for. You inspired the workhorse in me. You always told me that whatever I wanted to achieve in life I should pursue to my fullest abilities. But you also stressed that I should pursue something I love to do. That advice has been my North Star. You never judge me and are always there when I need advice. I would not be the man I am or have the career I have without your sage guidance over the years. From my early start in California to owning my own business in Vancouver, you have provided the very best advice and support along the way. You're the best.

Mom, you are the reason I am a chef today. Your passion for food and commitment to using the freshest ingredients to make incredibly delicious homemade meals every night while I was growing up is what inspired my interest in food. While your love of good food provided a solid foundation for our family growing up, it was your immeasurable love of family and your positive bright light that sustained us. You are my biggest critic and my biggest fan. When I cook, I cook for you, just as now I write this book for you. I love you.

While the notion of writing a book may always have been in the back of my mind, there were people throughout my career who provided opportunities for me to develop my skills and who helped to define me as a chef. To all the culinary professionals I've had the good fortune to work with and learn from over the years, thank you.

There are so many people who made this book possible. Darrin Giblin is a long-time friend who introduced me to the world of television, which completely changed the direction of my career and life. I believe it's not just what you know, but who you surround yourself with that defines your journey. Darrin, I wouldn't be on television without your making the introductions and believing in me. This book is a result of the career-path changes you sparked. Thank you! Without your support, my journey would look very different.

The one and only PR rep, Michelle Lan, thank you for all your hard work with Temper. Without your hard work and your drive to get us on the map, Temper and television would not be possible. It was you that put us on TV segments for Temper that caught the eye of the TV world, which was the initial step moving in that direction.

Toby Dormer, you were the one who made the idea of writing a book get stuck in my head. Together we are a force to be reckoned with in the world of culinary television. You believed in my abilities from the start, you helped acquaint me with television expectations and realities, and together we've experienced incredible victories. You are a friend, a TV mentor and a partner. Toby, you're stuck with me from here on out. Let's take over the TV world!

Anna Olson is an icon in Canada and a go-to authority for many Canadians who aspire to bake their best. The process of developing this book began with you, Anna, and your kind introduction to our now-mutual publisher, Appetite by Random House. I've learned so much from you, both on and off the set of our television show, *The Great Chocolate Showdown*. You inspire the people around you and you set a high bar for excellence. I appreciate your knowledge and the professionalism with which you approach your work. You motivate me to bring my best every day.

Thank you, Robert McCullough and Zoe Maslow of Appetite by Random House, for making this dream of mine a reality. I have thoroughly enjoyed our collaboration and all the guidance you provided. This is just the beginning—I look forward to future collaborations. To the designer of the book, Kelly Hill: you brought my vision to life. Everything you have designed in the book, I couldn't have imagined—the book is a piece of art, just like the food portrayed throughout each chapter. Thank you.

To my incredible team at Temper Chocolate & Pastry, thank you for all you bring to the shop every day and for making it possible for me to step away to put this book together.

To all the people behind the scenes who worked to make sure the recipes and content of the book were on point, thank you.

I want to sincerely thank everyone who has believed in me, and in this book. You are the reason I push myself every day. Thank you.

Index